M000034317

| CHILDFAITH |

ChildFaith

Experiencing God and Spiritual

Growth with Your Children

Donald Ratcliff

| *&* |

Brenda Ratcliff

CASCADE *Books* · Eugene, Oregon

CHILDFAITH
Experiencing God and Spiritual Growth with Your Children

Copyright © 2010 Donald Ratcliff and Brenda Ratcliff. All rights reserved. Except for brief quotations in critical publications or reviews, no part of this book may be reproduced in any manner without prior written permission from the publisher. Write: Permissions, Wipf and Stock Publishers, 199 W. 8th Ave., Suite 3, Eugene, OR 97401.

Cascade Books
An Imprint of Wipf and Stock Publishers
199 W. 8th Ave., Suite 3
Eugene, OR 97401

www.wipfandstock.com

ISBN 13: 978-1-60608-552-3

All Scripture quotations, unless otherwise indicated, are taken from the HOLY BIBLE, NEW INTERNATIONAL VERSION®. NIV®. Copyright © 1973, 1978, 1984 by International Bible Society. Used by permission of Zondervan. All rights reserved.

Cataloging-in-Publication data:
_____

Ratcliff, Donald.
    Childfaith : experiencing God and spiritual growth with your children / Donald Ratcliff and Brenda Ratcliff.

    ISBN 13: 978-1-60608-552-3

    viii + 186 p. ; 23 cm. Includes bibliographical references.

    1. Children—Religious life. 2. Christian education of children. 3. Spiritual life—Christianity. I. Ratcliff, Brenda. II. Title.

BV4574 R37 2010
_____

Manufactured in the U.S.A.

This book is lovingly dedicated to our three wonderful children: John, Stephen, and Beth. You have taught us so much about parenting and have graciously overlooked our failures.

| Contents |

| ONE | # The Spiritual Growth and Experience of Children

CHILDREN ARE IMPORTANT TO GOD. They are important in every respect—emotionally, physically, and spiritually. If you look up the word *child* and other words that refer to kids in any Bible concordance, you will find literally hundreds of references to the little ones that God has given us to parent.[1] In two of the four gospels, the books of Matthew and Luke, almost every chapter mentions or at least alludes to children. Jesus repeatedly speaks of the high value of children when he tells his disciples, "Let the little children come to me, and do not hinder them, for the kingdom of God belongs to such as these" (Luke 18:16b). Then he makes a very unusual comment for his day and age: "I tell you the truth, anyone who will not receive the kingdom of God like a little child will never enter it" (18:17). He actually encourages adults to be like children spiritually!

Before we had children, Don finished a graduate degree in educational psychology, taught several college classes in child development, studied children's spiritual development for a number of years, and taught every age range of children (helping in the nursery would come later!). Brenda had completed a degree in Christian education, taught teacher-training workshops in churches, and taught every age range of children as well. We often served together in leading the youth program at our church, and even taught successive levels of Sunday school at the same time. Yet we were still amazed at what we did not know about kids when we became parents.

We watched our three children grow and develop spiritually, and even had the privilege of leading each of them to Christ. We read them

---

1. Two excellent resources that describe what the Bible says about children are Bunge, *The Child in the Bible*; and Zuck, *Precious in His Sight*.

Bible stories, held discussions with them about spiritual matters, and celebrated the biblical holidays with them. We studied, prayed regularly for our children, and talked with friends and experts about children's spiritual experiences and development. As a result, we found a wide variety of ways to help children prepare for, begin, continue, and deepen their relationship with Christ.

We are deeply grateful for the positive influence of our parents and teachers, who taught us a great deal about the Bible and God. Their support and encouragement at every point in our lives have deeply impacted our thinking and personal experience of God. This is not to say they were perfect. We sometimes wish they had helped us understand more about how to experience God and how to walk with God in everyday life, yet we are grateful they were good examples and were always willing to talk about spiritual matters. Now that our children are grown, we see our own mistakes; parenting is a very humbling task. But in the process of our experience as parents, as well as Don's professional study of spiritual development, we learned much about what it means to help children spiritually, and that learning is a never-ending process.

This book is intended to help you guide your children in a closer relationship with God, by reflecting upon research, study, and relevant experiences of parents like you. We know you want your youngsters to love and experience God, and grow in their spiritual lives. We would like to be your companions in helping your children grow spiritually. We hope our suggestions, at least some of them, will prove to be helpful to you.

A word of warning is in order. Not every suggestion we make fits every parent or every child. Because children and parents are so different, we offer a number of alternative methods that can lead to the same goal—spiritual growth and aliveness for your child. Please do not try to do everything in this book! It is far too much for one parent, or even two parents, to try to accomplish! Instead, we encourage you to consider the many possibilities we share here, then choose what fits you and your children. We will try to help you make these choices wisely, but it is even more important to ask God to guide. Pray for discernment as you read. Some of the suggestions may be unrealistic for parents who work full time. Even a stay-at-home parent cannot be expected to do every suggested activity. We know how busy two working parents can be, so you may find that only a few of the ideas are even in the realm of possibility. We encourage you to browse through the suggestions and try those that fit your personality and your specific children. You know them far better than we do, and you will probably have some idea of what can work, and of what is unrealistic for your situation.

If you are a single parent, or if you have a spouse that has no interest in helping your children spiritually, you may feel you are at a disadvantage. However, God loves single-parent families and the spiritually equivalent families where the spouse is uninvolved. God's love for you is reflected in his concern for widows and orphans throughout Scripture. Mothers and sometimes fathers must become the spiritual authority of their children when the spouse is absent physically or absent by lack of support.

Again, please don't feel you need to do everything listed here—it is just too much—but find what is useful for you and your situation, and feel free to adapt and modify suggestions as needed. And please don't consider this book a prescription for successful spiritual nurture—children have a free will and thus make their own decisions.

Don's Experience as a Child at a Christian Camp

The night was sweltering with August heat, and beads of sweat hung from the forehead of the camp preacher. He loudly pled for people to receive salvation, attempting to convince the hesitant congregation of the need for a new life and a closer walk with God. We sang several verses of "Just as I Am," and just as in previous years, one by one my friends slinked from the back row bench down the aisle, literally made of sawdust, to the hard, dark wooden railing they called an "altar" at the front of the large, rustic "tabernacle." The row of ten- and eleven-year-old boys dissolved until I was the only one left standing in the row. As I sang the last verse of "Just as I Am" for the fourth time, I realized that my going forward to join the others was inevitable. I knew I was no better than my friends, so once again I reluctantly, consciously dragged myself down to the front, once again bending my knees in the sawdust. Some of the sawdust stuck to my sweaty legs that stuck out from pant legs I had outgrown. I again bowed my head and inhaled the aging varnish that darkened the wood. There were others:

my friends, younger children, and a few adults. Some were crying, others praying, all seeking a new or at least better walk with God.

As I knelt down to shed some tears with my buddies at the altar, the senselessness of it all struck me. I had made this trip dozens of times over my few years of life: at camps, revival services, and other church-related events. Sometimes I went forward for salvation—because apparently it had not "stuck" since the last time—or a new infilling, or recommitment, or a victorious life, or sinless perfection, whatever the preacher offered that night. But the result was always the same—a few minutes on my knees, hanging onto that old altar. *But perhaps I should try just one more time*, I thought. After a few tears, I was called upon for a testimony of what happened. I saw smiles of encouragement from the congregation, as each of us took a turn telling what we thought had happened to us at the camp service, and finally the benediction freed us from the ordeal. I vowed that this time salvation would stick; this time I would really live the Christian life the way it was preached. But I also suspected that, like the last time, things in my life really wouldn't change.

Perfection and even the so-called normal Christian life eluded me. It seemed that God kept his distance, in spite of my attempts to serve him. I knew I was supposed to witness to unsaved people, but the people I witnessed to either were already Christians or had no interest in God. I tried to read the Bible, but it didn't seem to have much to do with school, home, and the rest of my life. How does an eleven-year-old live out the Christian faith?

You may have had experiences similar to mine when you were a child. Perhaps you know others who had such experiences. Regardless, I am sure you want to help your child in trying to define and live out a vital, growing relationship with God. I believe I have discovered some clearer direction in the quest to find what was missing during my childhood religious experiences. I think what I lacked was a genuine connecting with God on a regular basis and understanding faith as a spiritual journey. Perhaps what I needed was not repeated starts, beginning again and again, but rather a combination of learning about God, learning how to use those insights in practical ways, and direct experiences with God that were more than momentary beginnings. To accomplish these things, the home is far more influential than the church or the Christian school. Certainly a good church and Christian school can help build a strong foundation of faith, but they cannot replace a strong home environment; the research makes that clear.[2]

What Is Spiritual Development?

While spiritual growth influences many different areas of children's lives, it actually consists of two kinds of development or change. Spiritual *development* refers to age-related stages that occur as a child gets older; children think differently about spiritual matters with time because of the more general development occurring in all areas of their lives. The maturing of the brain influences this aspect of development a great deal. The second kind of change, spiritual *growth*, is the more global development that the Bible generally describes, in which an adult can be a spiritual infant and—in contrast—a small child may be very sensitive and responsive to God. This kind of growth is fairly independent of brain maturation. While people usually use *development* and *growth* interchangeably, in this chapter we make this distinction to emphasize their difference. As we will see, tracing these two kinds of development will help in defining what we mean by the term *spirituality*.

Stage-Centered Spiritual Development

Children often think quite differently from teenagers and adults due to their age and the related maturation of the brain. It is not just that youngsters think at a less complex level, but the kind of thinking can also be different. Many researchers have investigated how the thinking of kids changes as they grow older. Some of this research has even examined how their concepts of religion and faith shift with age and maturity. Most of the research on spiritual development builds on the theories of the famous child-development specialist Jean Piaget.[3] Piaget stated

2. Kenneth Hyde's book *Religion in Childhood and Adolescence* includes dozens of research studies that make this point vividly, describing schools and churches not only in the United States but in many other areas of the world as well. We will speak more on this in chapter 11.

3. Jean Piaget's books are very difficult reading even for experts in child development. If you want to study the details of his stages, check Catherine Stonehouse's *Joining Children on the Spiritual Journey* or any standard child-development textbook. Again, keep in mind that Piaget did not study spiritual development but rather mental development, and thus his stages may not fit children's spiritual development in every respect.

that preschoolers think more intuitively, rather than logically thinking through things. At about age five to seven, youngsters first begin to think logically about tangible objects, even when the objects are absent. It is not until about age ten or twelve that kids think abstractly about intangible things like justice and mercy, Piaget concluded.

Similarly, children gradually develop more sophisticated concepts of God, prayer, and other aspects of faith. For example, researchers have found that preschoolers' ideas about God tend to be that of a magician who grants their every wish if they merely ask in the right way. In contrast, school-aged children are likely to see him as a Superman who is bigger and better than other human beings, but not fundamentally different. Children can come to understand that God is omniscient (all knowing) by about age six or seven. By age eight they begin to understand the omnipotence (all-powerfulness) of God, but it probably will be several more years before they begin to appreciate the omnipresence of God (God's being everywhere at all times). Concepts of prayer, the Bible, and other ideas related to God tend to follow a similar progression.[4]

Age differences in understanding faith-related topics are important to keep in mind.[5] Speaking simply about God and his love for children is more appropriate for preschoolers than attempting to teach abstract doctrines. Discussing things that are too complicated at a given age will usually produce confusion, boredom, and a dislike for spiritual topics.

While understanding the differences in the ways children think at various ages is important, you need to be careful not to think your youngster is necessarily limited by the stages that experts describe. Spiritual stages only show what is typical or average for a child when tested or questioned in some way. You could ask, would the stages of child development look different if kids were tested in other ways? Research can give us clues as to how children change in their thinking about faith, but not every child follows the patterns in the books, and if a youngster has different experiences—such as experiences of God or loving encourage-

4. Dozens, perhaps hundreds, of research studies have attempted to trace this progression. The most complete summary to date is Kenneth Hyde's book.

5. One of the best books summarizing these differences for parents is Stonehouse, *Joining Children on the Spiritual Journey*. I give some attention to these changes in Meier and Ratcliff, *Raising Your Child*, which can be found online in two sections at http://www.don.ratcliffs.net/raisingchild/part1.pdf and at http://www.don.ratcliffs.net/raisingchild/part2.pdf. For a more general view of children's mental development, see any standard child-development textbook.

ment from a parent—it is possible they will be more advanced. Children may differ because of different rates of development as well as because of differences in training.

For example, one of our children at about age five was on a church retreat with us. One evening, as we sat staring at a bonfire, our son remarked, "The fire is like Jesus on the cross, and the stones around the fire are like the people looking up at Jesus." We were amazed at this spontaneous comment, because we realized that the abstract thinking involved was not supposed to develop until the pre-teen years, according to Piaget and other researchers. Similarly, Jerome Berryman tells of children who even during the preschool years spontaneously compare themselves with the sheep tended by the Good Shepherd in the biblical parable.[6] Again this reflects an abstract level of thinking that many researchers say could not develop until age eleven or twelve at the earliest, and not even by the end of the teen years for some. Clearly Piaget's theory and the research of spiritual development influenced by his theory are not the last words on children's mental and spiritual development. Indeed, major gaps can arise between what children think spontaneously (reflected in our son's comments and in the preschoolers Berryman studied) and their explanations of specific physical tasks (which Piaget studied), as well as their responses to questions from other researchers. When researchers interview children, they depend upon children's language for their data. Yet talking may not reflect all that youngsters learn, because a child may have language limitations, and because we tend to listen more to our kids' responses to our instruction than to their spontaneous comments.

Thus stages provide one perspective of spiritual development, but we need to hedge on whether specific stages sufficiently describe children's spirituality. Parents and teachers who teach their children about spiritual issues may speed up their development in some respects, and the child's personal experience in applying what has been taught may also influence that development. When teaching is infused into everyday life, such as parents expressing amazement at a beautiful sunset, or awe at how God made us the spiritual progress of the child may be enhanced.

An overemphasis upon stages and the limitations of children's thinking can easily result in condescension. Children sense when adults are demeaning them, such as when adults laugh at cute but obviously

6. Jerome Berryman's book is *Godly Play: A Way of Religious Education.*

wrong comments about God. We need to value the immaturity of children as a necessary path to maturity. But we must not wait until youngsters can talk with precision about their Christian walk before we affirm the journey. Rather, we can affirm their experience and understanding now, even with their imperfections. By our affirming a child's current experience, in spite of immaturity, she or he can have the confidence to grow and mature.

On the other hand, there is something to the idea of phases or stages through which children pass in spiritual development. The stages that researchers describe do represent something that happens for many children. The famous Alfred Edersheim even suggests that the different Hebrew words that refer to children in the Old Testament and later in the Mishnah imply such a progression:[7]

- *jelled/jaldah* refers to the newborn baby (used in reference to circumcision, which occurs on the eighth day after birth)

- *jonek* refers to the suckling babe not yet weaned

- *olel* is the baby who is still a suckling child but can also eat bread

- *gamul* technically means "completed" and refers to the weaned child, which occurred at the end of the second year and was celebrated by a feast

- *taph* refers to the clinging child, who the rabbis felt should be taught selected passages of Scripture by three years of age

- *elem/almah* means "firm and strong," thus referring to the child who can read the Bible and attends school, which usually began between five and seven years of age.

- *naar* literally means "shakes himself free" and designates the youth who is expected to affirm the commandments at age thirteen through the Bar Mitzvah

- *bachur* is the "ripened one" or "warrior" who is married (usually between sixteen and eighteen for men, according to the rabbis) and pursues a trade (by age twenty, said the rabbis)

---

7. Edersheim, *Sketches of Jewish Social Life*, updated edition, chapter seven.

Spiritual Growth as a Process Unrelated to Age

Children can grow and develop in their spiritual lives in ways that do not depend upon age and mental abilities. Indeed, spiritual sensitivity may be stronger in younger children, and then can decrease as they move into the school years because peers and others tease them if they talk about God and spiritual experiences.[8]

Adults who become Christians are often marked by rapid growth with many changes in thought and action reflecting a major shift of priorities. By contrast, the changes that accompany salvation may not be major with a child, particularly with a young child, as there are not the years of living for the Enemy that have to be reversed. In children, spiritual growth is more likely to be gradual. You and your child are more likely to see growth in retrospect, as you look back on the subtle changes over several years of time, rather than in sudden shifts.

While growth involves change, it is also important that your children have both a desire for change and a degree of contentment with where they are spiritually. Your youngster should be open to God so that spiritual growth is more likely, yet there can also be a satisfaction that allows him or her to thank God for past spiritual growth. What complicates this is that sometimes we Christians glorify someone who has lived in the depths of sin and then makes dramatic changes when they become a Christian. Such individuals may be the focus of attention for special services at church and may make guest appearances on religious television programs. But this can raise questions for our children when they wonder why such dramatic changes have not occurred in their own lives. They may even question the authenticity of their salvation because they don't see the major differences that they hear in testimonies of others. We need to affirm to our children the importance of spiritual growth but also help them see that God accepts them here and now, complete with their flaws and rough areas, because it is by the righteousness of Christ that they are accepted by God (Rom 8). God more often makes subtle, gradual changes in the Christian child.

So what spiritual changes over time are to be expected in children? There are at least ten areas of life where this can occur. First, there is movement toward God prior to salvation, followed by a moment of

8. Hay and Nye, *The Spirit of the Child.* Brendan Hyde considers this problem in even greater depth in *Children and Spirituality*.

salvation or conversion, which involves a simple affirmation and commitment of life to God. After salvation there can be dramatic changes or small increments of change. We will examine the immediate steps leading to a child's salvation and the conversion experience in more detail in chapter 4.

Second, spiritual growth in your child is reflected in learning biblical content. Usually children learn the Bible in spirals, returning to the same ideas and stories of the Bible every few months or years, and having new insights and understandings because of additional experience and maturity since their previous exposure. When small children ask for the same story ten times in a row, they may be reflecting that spiral on a small scale. This is one reason why celebrating the biblical holidays each year can help your children understand progressively more about God and faith (see chapter 8).

Third, over time, your child's view of God, salvation, and other areas of theology are becoming clearer and—hopefully—more consistent with the Bible. Unfortunately, accurate views of spiritual matters do not guarantee a close walk with God; theology is intellectual while the walk with Christ is experiential. But ideally, your child will eventually hold a view of spiritual things that is accurate and will live out that truth in daily life. Because their mental capacity may be limited, children may not move quickly toward consistency and clarity in their comprehension of theology. Correction can result in different words being stated, but this is unlikely to create a new level of thinking for a youngster who is not yet capable of abstraction.

Spiritual formation is a fourth aspect of spiritual growth. This refers to your child's becoming more and more like Jesus Christ as his example is followed. Of course there are a few ways in which we are not to be like Christ, such as dying for the sins of the whole world. But in most respects children can move in the direction of Christ's perfect walk with God. It is possible that a small child could misconstrue the idea of imitating Christ, perhaps thinking she needs to wear a robe all the time! But if we emphasize attitudes and love, as well as doing what is right, this should make sense to kids.

Fifth, spiritual growth also refers to the child's loving God, praising God, and wanting more of God. These characteristics may be found to some extent in children, but parents need to be realistic. Video games are more likely to be appealing for a ten-year-old than an hour in prayer.

Yet with the right encouragement, children can develop a hunger for spiritual depth.

Spiritual growth entails increasing sensitivity to the Holy Spirit, learning to listen to God's voice, obeying what he says in the Bible and in the "still, small voice." Children sometimes report hearing from God and being directed by God in ways that go beyond what they are taught. Yet some skeptical adults may attribute these to an active imagination. This sixth area of growth can be encouraged by using the imagination to picture God at work (more on this in chapter 5).

Seventh, spiritual growth is marked by what theologians call *sanctification*: becoming aware of an area of sin, confessing that sin, receiving God's forgiveness, and turning from that sin. This is something that children may find to be easy or difficult. Sometimes the difference is a matter of personality, but the phase of spiritual growth can also make a difference. The quick recognition of their own sin is a characteristic that children can acquire, but they need careful guidance to avoid excessive guilt in this area.

Spiritual growth is also faith development, the eighth aspect of spiritual growth. One helpful age-related stage theory of faith development is that of James Fowler.[9] The degree of faith should increase as your child grows in Christ. As your child experiences Jesus as a dependable and loving Savior, faith increases. Unfortunately some children have parents who do not act in a trustworthy manner, and thus it is harder for them to have faith in God. Fortunately this can change with time, but it may be a slow and difficult process. (See chapters 2 and 3 for more on what a parent can do to encourage trust and thus, later, faith in God.)

A ninth area of spiritual growth is moral development. Again stage theories that describe different kinds of reasoning about moral issues at various ages can provide some insight,[10] yet for the Christian, moral growth centers on the decisions your child makes and the resulting actions taken, not just on moral reasoning. A child's conscience can be too sensitive, causing the child to feel guilt about things not condemned in

9. The best known of these is James Fowler's theory. See his *Stages of Faith*. I also appreciate Stonehouse's examination of this theory in relation to children. See Stonehouse, *Joining Children on the Spiritual Journey*, 145–68.

10. While Lawrence Kohlberg's theory has dominated this area (see Stonehouse's excellent summary and assessment of his work), other theorists have suggested very helpful ideas that are less stage focused. See, for example, Coles, *The Moral Life of Children*.

the Bible. Or the conscience may be underdeveloped, and as a result a child may not feel guilt for things that are morally wrong (more on this in chapter 3). Moral growth involves the conscience's becoming more sensitive to biblical standards, and with the child's actions reflecting that movement towards God's ideals. Yet at some point children need to develop a sensitivity to others who have more restrictive consciences, and to the degree possible must respect those convictions. As I Corinthians 8:9 states, "Be careful, however, that the exercise of your freedom does not become a stumbling block to the weak." Realizing that an action can be acceptable in God's sight but not the best thing to do because of another person's convictions may appear to be inconsistent or even incomprehensible to younger children. But older children are more likely to understand the overarching principle of avoiding some practices out of love for others, even though there is nothing wrong with doing those things (I John 3:11, 21).

Finally, spiritual growth involves the increased giving of one's time in service to others—spiritually, materially, and in other ways—so that others are encouraged, live more healthfully, and receive a witness of faith. Family projects that involve service to others are associated with a strong and growing faith in children.[11] When you consider all of the above components of spiritual growth (and it is possible that we have missed some), it is clear that spiritual growth is complex and highly idealistic. But rest assured, you are capable of helping your child spiritually. It may not be easy, but God is waiting to help you.

It is important to note that it is God, not we as parents, who initiates spiritual growth, and that it is reflected outwardly as well as within the person.[12] Telling your children your faith story—including both your experience of salvation and aspects of your subsequent walk with God—including changes and redirection by God—will help them understand that not everything is expected to be perfect instantly.

As you have probably heard, use the teachable moments when your child asks a question; don't wait for a more convenient time. It may be that God prompted your child to ask that difficult question. It can be more important to talk for a few minutes in the car before you go into the grocery store than to do the grocery shopping at that moment. A follow-up at bedtime may be good, but by then the child's mind will probably be

11. Roehlkepartain, *The Teaching Church*, 170.

12. Stonehouse, *Joining Children on the Spiritual Journey*, 22, 24–25.

on other things. When a discussion is inconvenient, perhaps you need to ask yourself whether the child's spirituality is as important as the task at hand. We suspect that much of the time we convince ourselves that the child can wait until later, and then either forget to follow up or are not able to connect with the child later. The rule of thumb for working with our children is that things are better caught than taught, actualized and not merely vocalized, imitated rather than imposed, depicted but not inflicted.

Again, this may be familiar advice to you, but be honest if you do not know the correct answer to a child's question; that is far better than giving an answer that turns out to be in error, and that thus undermines your credibility.[13] Parents need to talk about God and spiritual experiences in the midst of everyday life, just as Jesus once said (perhaps on a hillside covered by lilies), "Consider now the lily" to teach about freedom from worry (Matt 6:28). The famous passage in Deuteronomy (6:6–7) underscores the important principle of embedding the spiritual in the day-to-day experience of life with children: "These commandments I give you today are to be upon your hearts. Impress them on your children. Talk about them when you sit at home and when you walk along the road, when you lie down and when you get up."

Even though we speak of infusing or embedding spirituality into daily life, in reality we are not imposing something foreign to our children. Instead, we are highlighting and commenting on the spiritual dimension that really exists. To point out spiritual aspects of what occurs, we are affirming the unseen world that is connected to the seen world. We should always remember that we only "see in part" (1 Corinthians 13); there is a spiritual world all around us, whether we are aware of it or choose to ignore it.

We are impressed that God does not want our children to be prepared for a test but rather for a relationship. Yet sometimes parents teach their children about God, spirituality, or faith as if they must pass an exam. Too often the church has taught children Bible trivia, or worse, merely tried to entertain them[14] but has neglected the important place of the spiritual and the relational. It is not wrong to teach biblical

---

13. Ibid., 27–28, 37–38, 67, 135.

14. Our colleague and friend Scottie May particularly sensitized us to these faulty goals in children's ministry. See her book, *Children Matter*, coauthored with Beth Posterski, Catherine Stonehouse, and Linda Cannell.

content, and we will consider this in greater detail in chapter 6. Parents can teach children a story or a parable by helping them experience the story through enactment or through taking fieldtrips (see chapter 10), but parents might also suggest another level of experience, encouraging children to personalize the story as coming from God. God speaks to children, sometimes through stories, and sometimes in other ways. Sometimes God uses language to speak to children, but at times he uses more direct ways of communicating with them.

The Spiritual Experiences of Children

While the spiritual growth and development of our children is a central concern, we must not overlook the importance of their spiritual experiences. Just as faith without works is dead (Jas 2:26, KJV), so too a faith without spiritual experience tends to be lifeless and sterile. Indeed, without spiritual experience a life of faith is more likely to be merely religion rather than an active relationship with God. Sometimes the distinction is made that we need to teach about God yet not neglect the experience of God.

Yet when we begin to talk about children's spiritual experiences, this can mean many different things to different people. Spirituality is an incredibly popular topic today. Almost every talk-show host brings in guests to speak on the issue—and this is particularly the case with Oprah Winfrey. Many popular books, television shows, movies, and even popular music have strong spiritual themes. Over the last few decades much of the Western world has moved from ignoring spiritual experience to embracing or at least seriously discussing spirituality in its many forms.

It is the many forms of spirituality that should concern us. Everything from odd variations of Christianity dismissed centuries ago as clearly heresy to occult practices are heralded as legitimate options. Many Americans delight in choosing aspects of different spiritualities that they find appealing, blending together what they see as the best of different faiths and traditions, from notions about a mother goddess to appealing statements made by Jesus. It is only natural for such individuals to pass on such a hodgepodge of faith to their children. Similarly, school teachers might encourage kids to create their own mixture of beliefs. What is most crucial to note is that spiritual experience can be accompanied by accurate understandings and reflect a vital relationship with God, or similar experiences can be associated with faulty and even antibiblical understandings.

What do we mean by the phrase "spiritual experiences of children"? In this book we will examine what is becoming one of the most common understandings of this idea, see how it fits with Christian understandings, and then also will see how the spiritual experiences of Christians, including Christian children, are distinct from other spiritual experiences.

The Numinous Experiences of Children

From the earliest years of life, youngsters apparently have experiences of awe and wonder when time seems to stand still and they become thoroughly engrossed with a sight, sound, or thought. Rebecca Nye conducted research with school-aged children in England and found that such experiences were as much perceptual as they were emotional;[15] such experiences changed how the child perceived the world. Spiritual experience was a common activity for most of the children studied, regardless of their religious views, and even occurred among children who had no religious faith.

Early in the twentieth century, German theologian Rudolf Otto described somewhat similar experiences, albeit with adults rather than with children, and concluded they were common to all religions.[16] However, he emphasized that the Christian faith was the highest and most developed religion, and he was a practicing Christian. Otto called such experiences encounters of the numinous, which cannot be taught but can be awakened by the individual and perhaps (in the case of children) by others, such as parents. While the numinous experience can be described, ultimately it cannot be understood from a purely rationalistic perspective, because "it is the experience of the other, the holy, the incomprehensible—of God."[17]

---

15. Hay and Nye, *The Spirit of the Child*. Nye's description is more complex than what is described here, as I have chosen to focus on those aspects of the experience that other researchers have tended to emphasize as well. Compare, for example, the experience of "flow" described by Csikszentmihaly in *Flow: The Psychology of Optimal Experience*.

16. Otto, *The Idea of the Holy*.

17. Spiceland, "The Numinous," 783.

In many ways, what Otto describes fits what the researchers say about children's spirituality. Otto emphasizes how many biblical descriptions of spiritual experience fit the concept of the numinous, and that such experiences reveal a hidden dimension of life: the world of the spirit, where God and his angels (as well as the Enemy and his angels) dwell and interface with human beings, whether we realize it or not.

The numinous experience reveals the biblical truth that deep within the core of every child is a spirit, the self that lives within and controls the brain and body. This part of the child is connected to another realm, the spiritual realm. From an evangelical Christian perspective, numinous experiences are a way that God attempts to draw non-Christian children to himself as he desires to enter into a relationship with youngsters through the death of God's only son, Jesus Christ. It is also possible that the Enemy, Satan, may imitate the numinous experience through the excitement or pleasure of sinful activities and supernatural experiences associated with the occult and other false religions.

Thus when we speak of "spiritual experiences," or the experience of the numinous, we are emphasizing the very real realm of the spirit, and God's influence (or the Enemy's false imitation of that influence) upon the child's inner self, the human spirit. Christian children have the Holy Spirit within, which produces a unique connection to God, as the Holy Spirit is one person of the triune God.

Solomon wrote in Ecclesiastes 3:11: "He has made everything beautiful in its time. He has also set eternity in the hearts of men; yet they cannot fathom what God has done from beginning to end." The experience of the numinous produces awe and wonder in children because it is an expression of the eternity in the hearts of all human beings. While Augustine said we are all made for God,[18] and Pascal described a void within the person that only God can fill,[19] it is important to note that the spiritual experiences of children reflect the eternity in the child's heart,

18. "You have made us for yourself, and our heart is restless until it rests in you." Saint Augustine, *Confessions* 1.1 (trans. Henry Chadwick) 3.

19. Pascal, *Penses*, trans. Honor Levi, 52. While this phrase is often quoted as including the English word *vacuum*, no recent translation of this book could be located that uses the word *vacuum* here. In the cited translation, the exact quotation is, "Man tries unsuccessfully to fill this void with everything that surrounds him, seeking in absent things the help he cannot find in those that are present, but all are incapable of it. This infinite abyss can be filled only with an infinite, immutable object, that is to say, God himself."

the fact they are made for God, and that kids also have a void or spiritual longing that can only be filled and fulfilled by God. Thus spirituality is not something foreign we are imposing upon children; it is integral to their very being.

We love the Chronicles of Narnia. These seven books authored by C. S. Lewis resonate deeply, and as we read them to our children, they resonated deeply with them as well. Indeed all three of our now-grown children have their own sets of the books. As a twelve-year-old, our daughter watched the videos of the series each night as she went to sleep until the tapes wore out! The more recent film versions are even more captivating.

What is it that resonates with our children from these books? We believe it is the affirmation of an alternate realm with talking beavers and horses, and of course Aslan, the lion who is clearly a picture of Christ. The Narnia stories resonate with the reality that we all live in two realms: the everyday world and another world that in some ways resembles Narnia. In the spirit realm, Christ has taken away the cold of perpetual winter brought on by the White Witch (the Enemy) because the death of the Lion of Judah is a substitute for all of us who deserve death, and now the Lion is resurrected, bringing spring, new life, and a new connectedness to God through Christ. The Chronicles of Narnia give us the heart of the gospel as well as the central truth that we live in two realms at the same time.

Thus to have spiritual experiences is an indication that a spiritual world exists simultaneously with the material world of sights, sounds, smells, and touch. This spiritual dimension intersects with the natural world and ultimately transcends it. Experiences of awe and wonder may very well reflect a touching of that spiritual world. While this sounds very abstract, and it is rather abstract, the older child who has watched *Star Trek* or similar science-fiction programs may already understand the idea of multiple dimensions. You can point out that the spiritual world is a bit like that except that we are not as knowledgeable about the spiritual world as these shows suggest. To a considerable extent, the unseen world is a great mystery, although the Bible does give us some glimpses of what it is like. We know from Scripture that there the unseen world is alluring (and thus the ban on séances and witchcraft in the Old Testament). It can be dangerous, and thus the need for spiritual armor (Ephesians 6). Thus today's "cafeteria-style" spirituality is particularly dangerous, as one is like to confuse the holy and profane, deity and demonic, as well as the real and illusory.

Christian Spiritual Experiences of Children

While Christian children have experiences of awe and wonder much like those of non-Christian youngsters, some spiritual experiences are distinctive to Christians. Perhaps most obvious is the experience of salvation. When youngsters accept Christ as Savior, there is a change of heart, and each becomes a "new creature" (2 Cor 5:17, KJV). Genuine conversion involves a turning, a change in perspective, and this may or may not involve a highly emotional experience. It makes sense that eventually, if not immediately, there would be awe and wonder that God would love them so much that he would die for them, and that he wants to enter a relationship with them. But sometimes this realization may not come until much later. Regardless, salvation is an experience (substantive change occurs spiritually as the Holy Spirit enters the child, cleanses the youngster of sin, and makes a "new creature") as well as a decision, whether or not it is emotional or filled with wonder.

Subsequent spiritual experiences are also distinctive to Christian children. The Holy Spirit produces a sensitivity to God that probably was not there before, which brings illumination (insight beyond what is humanly possible without God). There may be other kinds of spiritual experiences that are distinctively Christian as well. Indeed, the basic fabric of a child's nature is deeply embedded in mystery.[20]

For example, educator Peter McLaren, an admittedly Marxist, postmodern non-Christian, researched children in a Catholic school and noted what he describes as a "sanctity state" during chapel at the school. The children's reverence and sense of the holy struck McLaren as very different from how the youngsters acted and thought during the rest of the day. Their comments emphasized that this was an unusual mental and emotional state, and that they saw God as personally involved in the experience.[21]

20. Marty, *The Mystery of the Child.*

21. McLaren, *Schooling as a Ritual Performance*, 2nd ed. While McLaren and Rudolf Otto are at opposite extremes of belief, they described spiritual experience in very similar terms.

Do Christian children have more spiritual experiences than non-Christian children? Certainly our children are more likely to have the distinctively Christian experiences we have noted here, but we are not sure they will automatically have more of the general numinous experiences. Some churches tend to discourage such experiences by their emphasis upon a mental acceptance of Christ, cognitive understandings of the Bible, and agreement on beliefs. Some churches actively discourage any kind of spiritual experience. At least in theory, Christians should be more sensitive to God's majesty in creation and thus may have both more general numinous experiences and distinctively Christian spiritual experiences. Indeed, perhaps the more general experiences become distinctively Christian experiences by adding God as the object of the awe and wonder experienced, and by the focus of inward or outward praise that can result.

As parents, we can encourage our children to be open to spiritual experiences, recognizing that God is the initiator, and kids are to be willing participants. On the other hand, we must also be cautious that we do not make spiritual experiences the objects of desire. To seek the experience instead of seeking God is to make the experience an idol. It must also be admitted that artificial, fabricated, self-initiated experiences can actually get in the way of God's presence. We should teach our children to be open and receptive to God but also bow to his sovereign will in whether or not such experiences occur.

Encouraging Children's Spiritual Experiences

How can we encourage children to be receptive to spiritual experiences from God? Fortunately it is often fairly easy to encourage the Godward redirection of a child's awe and wonder. If the child is impressed with the beauty of the Grand Canyon, the parent can simply say, "Isn't this a wonderful thing that God has made? Let's thank him and tell him how great he is to have created this." The goal of such comments is not to build good theology, although hopefully that will result. The goal is to encourage the child to infuse praise and gratefulness in the spiritual experience. The initial object of our awe and wonder is the Grand Canyon, but how much greater should that awe and wonder be when your child realizes that she personally knows the Creator of the Grand Canyon, and also understands that he gives us the great privilege of seeing and enjoying his creation when we visit this marvel.

While we may conceptually infuse God into moments of spiritual experience, at times we may need to simply let God do his work and not try to explain things to our child. Catherine Stonehouse, echoing the thoughts of Jerome Berryman, suggests that adults who teach in the church sometimes interrupt a child's spiritual experience to talk about theology or the Bible.[22] Specifically she describes how the story of the Good Shepherd can produce a spiritual experience for the child, and often children need time and space to reflect on the personal meaning as they sense awe and wonder at their being like the sheep and God's being like the shepherd loving the sheep. Parents need to be sensitive to when the child needs to be allowed without interruption to experience God, biblical content, or perhaps other things that produce awe and wonder. Be sensitive to the leading of the Holy Spirit.

As mentioned earlier, children have spiritual experiences long before they can be taught about them. In a sense you can consider your teaching as giving a language to the experience.[23] Of course it is important to teach in such a way that children do not depreciate their earlier, more naïve experiences.

Preparation for spiritual experience is valuable for children, especially in helping them direct that experience Godward. This in part involves overt teaching about experiencing God, listening to God, talking to God, and allowing God to change them. Perhaps the most important thing to convey is that it is good to have such experiences, and that they are a natural and positive part of a relationship with Christ. Part of the reason to do this is to help "vaccinate" the child against the perils of later peer and adult pressure to ignore or avoid spiritual experiences. Youngsters need our affirmation of spiritual experiences.

By contrast, if your child mentions something God told them, or a special experience that was very meaningful, it may be very unpleasant for them to receive a lecture on theology in response. Affirm their comments, even if part of what they say lacks theological sophistication. Mistaken theology can be corrected later; the important thing is that the

22. The reference here is to Stonehouse's videotape titled *Children's Worship*. A short segment is available online at http://childfaith.net/stonehouse.html. Also see Berryman, *Godly Play*.

23. Berryman, *Godly Play*, 144–54.

child understands that it is wonderful for them to have had a meaningful spiritual encounter with God, nature, or people.

As children grow older, during the school years, they can be taught more about spiritual experiences so they will understand them more completely. Generally this will take the form of short teachings that may be repeated and elaborated. The important thing is that the child engage in the discussion, asking questions and sharing experiences and understandings. Children need dialogue.

Older children may also be taught about a degree of control that we have over spiritual experience. For example, when deeply enjoying a piece of music, one can elect to hear only the notes, words, and other musical elements, or one can give way to worship and a potential encounter with God. In other words, we can control how far the experience takes us (1 Cor 14:32). We cannot command God to create a spiritual experience. However, we can ask, and we can be ready to receive. Rabbi Shlomo Carlebach commented, "Full experiences with God can never be planned or achieved. They are spontaneous moments of grace, almost accidental." When Bo Lozoff asked, "If God-realization is just accidental, why do we work so hard doing all these spiritual practices?" the rabbi replied, "To be as accident-prone as possible."[24]

You may also want to explain to your child that spiritual experiences can change the way we look at the world. We may become more conscious of clouds, the beauty of mountains, and how much we love other people, because of special times of awe and wonder related to these experiences. Take the time to stop and look at the things of nature so that you and your child can reflect upon their importance and beauty.

We can also make room for spiritual experiences through daily rituals at bedtime or at the dinner table. While these rituals are important times of teaching, be sure to allow time for children to reflect after the teaching, which may result in spiritual experience. (We will consider these issues in detail in chapter 7.) Similarly family fieldtrips can also provide opportunities to make room for such experiences (see chapter 10).

Spiritual experiences may also be the product of the spiritual disciplines. These include special times of extended prayer, fasting, meditation, and the like. Only recently has the possibility of children's

24. Lozoff, *It's a Meaningful Life*, 23–24.

participating in such activities been considered.[25] Certainly some of the spiritual disciplines are more appropriate than others for children. For example, if an older child expresses an interest in fasting, we think it is appropriate for the child to miss a meal or two and give that time to prayer and reflection. But while we think it would be acceptable to talk about the disciplines, we never think it appropriate to require or to force the child into such practices. The Holy Spirit needs to be allowed to draw children into the disciplines. Too often parents and pastors try to assume the role of the Holy Spirit. We must work with, not try to replace, the Holy Spirit in the lives of others, including our children.

The form of spiritual experiences can vary a great deal. Children may find that God may be heard in the quietness, even as Elijah found God in the "still small voice" (1 Kgs 19:12, KJV). Harvard University professor Robert Coles discovered in his research that children claim to hear God's voice, and that they sometimes talk to God but do not associate this with prayer.[26] Youngsters also sense a response from God in answers to prayers. Catherine Stonehouse, a teacher at Asbury Theological Seminary, describes the importance of a child's quiet reflection, a condition that can be fostered by setting aside a special place for worship and reflection.[27] By contrast, children also may experience God in a lively context and thus show exuberant praise through shouting, singing, dancing, and other high-activity-level actions. Interestingly, a systematic biblical study of the words *worship* and *praise* reflects a similarly broad spectrum of spiritual experience in the Scriptures.[28]

25. Valerie Hess and Marti Watson Garlett consider this topic in detail in *Habits of a Child's Heart* A classic book on the subject of spiritual disciplines in general is Richard Foster's *Celebration of Discipline*, rev. ed. We also appreciate Klaus Issler's wonderfully readable book on the topic of friendship with God, which includes some very practical ideas related to the spiritual disciplines as well as other valuable perspectives on relating to God: *Wasting Time with God: A Christian Spirituality of Friendship with God.*

26. Coles, *The Spiritual Life of Children*. Stonehouse, *Joining Children on the Spiritual Journey*, 141–42, also cites Coles in this respect, noting that God does not just tell children what they have been taught, but also calms their fears and helps direct their actions.

27. See Stonehouse, *Joining Children on the Spiritual Journey*, who adapts Jerome Berryman's more liturgical approach with children for more mainstream evangelical use. Also see her videotape, mentioned above.

28. For example, the Hebrew words translated "praise" can reflect thanksgiving, adoration, or loud celebration in various passages. They can also imply kneeling, extending the hands, singing, or playing a musical instrument. We need to encourage our children to experience the full spectrum of worship revealed in the original languages of Scripture.

Children also need to see worship and praise as a daily activity, even when a spiritual experience does not result. This can be a part of a ritual bedtime prayer, dinner-table devotion, or other regular activity. Yet your child also needs to realize that the goal is not to let that daily activity be the only time with God; rather the goal is to experience daylong affirmation of God. This is probably too much to expect of children, but ultimately the walk with God should be continual, punctuated with brief times of prayer and praise throughout all activities.[29]

Children need to see their spiritual lives as more than a series of spiritual experiences; it also involves learning about God. Likewise while learning and growing are important, the Christian life can be rather bleak seen only as acquiring information and as learning to avoid certain bad behaviors. At the most fundamental level, spiritual growth and experience are two complementary aspects of what is meant by having a relationship with Christ. Life's spiritual journey also is an ongoing learning experience that changes one's thinking and behavior. In other words, the journey involves moving from one place to another but also experiencing God during the journey. The process of movement (spiritual growth) is gradual. But the journey also includes many points of interest: the spiritual experiences along the way. Those experiences may occur daily for some Christians, less often for others. Just as major cities are important points along a road, some spiritual experiences are major influences in the spiritual life of a child—remembered weeks, months, or even years later. But not every spiritual experience is so intense. Others are minor, such as listening to a favorite worship song that draws us into God's presence. These are more like the small towns and intersections on an interstate highway. They are to be appreciated; yet they quickly disappear from view. Children need the ongoing relationship and connection with God; the overall process is a journey, but they also need at least an occasional spiritual experience that punctuates the journey.

Conclusion

Join us as we consider the exciting journey parents make with their children, from birth up to the teen years. Throughout this journey we will examine many possible ideas and practices for spiritual development.

29. See Issler, *Wasting Time with God*, 230–34, for more on this practice.

But, again, you are not expected to do everything listed here; you are in the best place to decide what will work best for you, your child, and your situation. The decisions you make, as well as the degree of your own personal involvement with your children, can influence whether or not your children grow up to love God and live for him.

While I (Don) have written, coauthored, and edited a number of books prior to this one, I sensed special guidance during this work. Sometimes I wondered if my hands on the keyboard were responding more to God than to myself. God has blessed me marvelously in all of life, but this guidance in writing was an unexpected blessing. The mistakes either came from faulty listening on my part or reflect my struggle to hear when nothing was said.

We are grateful for the privilege of parenting our own three children and for their forgiveness for the many times we fell short. It seems like only yesterday that they were running through our home, leaving sneakers, Legos, books, and a host of dirty dishes and laundry. Now they are adults and soon may be parents themselves. We are proud of them. But even more, we are grateful to a heavenly Father who has been so patient with us and continues to "grow us" toward spiritual maturity.

| TWO |

Baby Faith

Forming Strong Roots of
Faith in Infancy

June looked at her newborn and was moved to tears. "Labor"—an apt word for the hard work she had just been through. But the delight of seeing this little one with whom she had shared her body made it all seem worthwhile: The tiny hands with tiny fingernails. Yes, all five fingers were on each hand. And the amazing toes with tiny toenails. Yes, they were all there too. "What a miracle birth is," she thought. Then the infant's eyes met hers. She smiled, and the baby responded with rapt attention. June thought she saw the beginnings of a smile in return. She began to wonder, "What can I do to encourage my baby to have faith in God and live for God?"

Before Birth: Preparing for the Child's Spiritual Development

WE ARE CONVINCED THAT there are many important things that need to take place before a baby is born, spiritual preparation for the child's entry into the outside world. God is at work in the child's world prior to birth. As Scripture states, God intricately "knits" the child in the mother's womb (Ps 139:13). The metaphor is a striking one, especially when one considers the fact that many ancient cultures believed that the baby is preformed in the father's body, and sexual intercourse only planted the preformed baby into the mother's body for the purpose of growth. Instead the biblical metaphor suggests that God creates the child in phases, just as one knits a sweater one area at a time. Research in the last decades of the twentieth century using tiny cameras inside mothers' bodies has not only shown us the beauty and grandeur of that knitting, but has established the different phases of physical development in the womb. For example, the central nervous system (the spinal cord and tiny brain) develops earlier than other parts of the body.[1]

What can parents do to prepare for the spiritual nurture of their child prior to birth? Certainly they can pray for their child. Prayer is important at every phase of the child's development, but prayer for parents' own preparation as well as for the baby's protection needs to begin early. A good friend of ours, now a clinical psychologist, told us that he often prayed for his children prior to birth by laying hands on his wife's abdomen as a symbolic connecting with the child. He was always very involved with his children throughout their developmental years, and we cannot help but think that this early spiritual contact through prayer may have played a part in solidifying his conviction to be involved in his children's lives.

Another area of need prior to birth is that parents take care to give the mother a positive experience during pregnancy. High stress and emotional turmoil can adversely influence the child. Avoiding contact with those who have communicable diseases, and avoiding most medications and contaminants can help the mother give the unborn child the best possible environment.[2] The goal is to provide for the child the best physical and emotional constitution that is reasonably possible.

The months before their child's birth is a good time for parents to reflect on their own spirituality. You can do a spiritual checkup and to work through past struggles and "baggage" that might hinder your ability to spiritually guide the child later on. If possible, reconcile with relatives, in-laws, co-workers, church folk, or others with whom you have had less than the best relationships. Problems in your relationships with other adults may be more difficult to deal with when the baby takes so much of your time, and those problems may translate to less emotional and physical energy to care for your child. It is easy when you are frustrated with other people to be less tolerant of or sensitive to your baby—and later, your child. You might be too tired to play with your baby (and later your child) because of problems at work, at church, or with relatives.

1. See Rathus, HDEV, 41.

2. For details, you may want to examine the book I coauthored with Paul Meier, *Raising Your Child* (online: www.don.ratcliffs.net/raisingchild/part1.pdf; and www .don.ratcliffs.net/raisingchild/part2.pdf).

Before the birth of your baby, you can work on the relationship with your spouse. Hopefully you have been working out the details of your life together well before the pregnancy, but if some rough areas still remain in that relationship, now is the best time to work on them. Once the baby comes, latent, hidden problems will likely come to the surface during the first months of feeding the baby in the middle of the night, during the endless diaper changes, and during the many other activities that accompany having a baby. Things will change eventually, and as the child grows you may have some time for yourselves again, but at any age children consume quite a bit of time. Take care of the obvious problems in your marriage before the baby arrives, and do your best to anticipate problems likely to surface after the birth of the baby. A healthy home life is a good preparation for a spiritually healthy child.

This is also a good time to investigate spiritually relevant resources for your baby and soon-to-be child. Check out your church nursery and the policies your church has for volunteers in the nursery and for children's programs. Who is it that cares for the babies—inexperienced teenage girls, or adults with have experience or training in child care? Are those in charge mature enough to assume responsibility for your child? Are police background checks required for child-care workers? What is the adult-child ratio in the nursery? A good ratio is at least one adult for every three babies, and never fewer than two adults total. If there are difficulties with your child, will those in charge contact you, and how can the nursery signal you in church? What are the hygienic procedures used in the nursery, and is a second adult present when diapers are changed or when a toddler or preschooler is taken to the bathroom? Are there indications that the church has a genuine concern for a baby's needs? Do the nursery and children's classrooms reflect a love and concern for youngsters, and do they have toys that encourage exploration, which can be a source of the awe and wonder characteristic of spiritual experience? If you plan to use day care, make similar investigations at that facility.

Investigate how your church feels about the presence of babies and small children in the main services. A long-standing debate continues about whether children should be with their parents in church, or if they should be in age-graded services of their own. Sometimes church policies are not written down, but an unwritten policy is presumed. Keep in mind that if you first elect to send your child to the nursery, you may change your mind and want to keep the child with you (or vice versa), so see if there is some flexibility in this matter. Even if the church permits children in the main services, does the church really celebrate children in the services, or are youngsters merely tolerated? Remember that Christ said that to welcome a child is like welcoming Christ himself (Luke 9:48).

Give consideration to the toys, music, and videos you want your child to play with, hear, or see when they get older. If you wait until they are three or four years old, it may be very easy to just buy products that are readily available and not to look carefully at the content. Even with Christian music and videos, both good and inferior products are available. It may be that the ancient Greeks were correct that good music enriches the soul. Take your time selecting toys and audio-visual materials, with concern for the moral and spiritual impact they will have on your child.

While you are at it, talk with your spouse or close friends about how involved they will be in the spiritual nurture of your child. Close friends prior to the birth of a child can quickly part ways if, say, one friend has a child and the other does not; you simply will not have as much in common with your friend after the child arrives. If your close friend also has a child, will differences in preferred child-rearing methods, or in the amount of television you allow your children to watch likely to cause discord or division? What kinds of things do you want to teach your child about your faith, and how will you teach them? The book you are reading may be a helpful source in this regard as you discover some ideas resonant with your personality and spiritual outlook. Seek to discuss with your spouse and friends the spiritual and faith practices and beliefs that are essential, about other formative activities that you are willing to try, and about still other practices and teachings that you do not want for your child. Reflect on your own spiritual training: what activities and ideas do you want to use with your child, and which do you plan to leave behind? This may even be a good time to brush up on your Bible knowledge, and even to develop a plan for discipline procedures, for teaching the Bible, for rituals and ceremonies you plan to observe, and so on. You may even want to consider innovative ideas such as a Christian bar mitzvah.[3]

3. I am grateful to Paul Meier for his thoughts on this topic, reflected in *Raising Your Child*. We tried this with one of our children during a church service but decided

In sum, the months prior to birth are an important time. Do not be content to just wait for the child and then see what you want to do for them spiritually. You probably will not have the time or energy then, so make the most of your pregnancy! No doubt you are physically preparing for your baby's arrival—painting the nursery, buying a crib, laundering all those tiny outfits. But don't forget to prepare spiritually as well!

Temperament and Faith

In the opening illustration of this chapter, June was right to be thinking that she may be able to influence her baby emotionally and spiritually. In the months after giving birth, June could influence the child positively or negatively in terms of belief and faith in God, as well as in other aspects of the child's emotional life; these influences that can stay with the child for many years to come.

For centuries some believed that a newborn baby was a blank slate, and that the experiences with other people in the environment completely determined the baby's disposition and behavior. Today this assumption is seriously questioned. Babies are born with temperaments that will influence their eventual personalities. While a number of different temperaments that have been suggested, perhaps the simplest approach to this topic is to describe the newborn as either an easy baby or a difficult baby, although temperament is actually more complicated than this.[4] Easy babies naturally enjoy being cuddled, and do not cry a great deal. By contrast, difficult babies seem to be unhappy much of the time and may even seem to resist the affection of the parent. Most babies are somewhere in between these extremes, but the inborn temperament will be quite clear within the first few weeks of life.

---

against it for our other children (see chapter 9). But we are glad we creatively tried different things, some of which we continued for all our children.

4. These descriptions are a bit oversimplified. The research indicates there are at least three aspects of temperament: activity level (highly active, moderately active, or relatively inactive), social level (highly social, moderately social, or relatively unsocial), and emotional level (a lot of negative emotions, a moderate amount of negative emotions, or relative lack of negative emotions). Interestingly, it appears that positive emotions are not related to inborn temperament but are a combination of environmental differences and personal choice. For a summary of the research on temperament, see a paper I did for my doctoral study: "Temperament in Childhood: Three Key Dimensions" (online: don.ratcliffs.net/conferences/temper.pdf).

Even though temperament is inborn, the parents and other adults will have an important influence upon the child. If those who care for the child follow the child's cues as to what is needed, even the difficult baby may become less difficult (although very unlikely to become an easy baby). Of course some difficult babies are that way because of physical problems that can be corrected. For example, one of our children was rather difficult for the first year or so of life. He seemed to sleep very little, taking very short naps of a few minutes, and rarely sleeping all night even by age two. He fussed and cried a great deal. At first doctors suspected a milk allergy, and so we gave him special milk. That seemed to help some, but he was still difficult. For months doctors made various suggestions, and we tried everything we (and they) could think of. Finally a doctor told us that his throat was partially blocked by large tonsils, adenoids, and other tissue. When he tried to sleep, the muscles of the throat relaxed, blocking off air to his lungs, thus his waking was his body's effort to sustain life. Surgery was scheduled, and almost immediately afterward we had a baby who slept all night and was happier (and so were we!).

Certainly temperament will influence personality and thus the way children are likely to live out the faith if they become Christians. One can think of the difficult baby becoming the skeptical or legalistic Christian while the easy baby might become a more easygoing Christian. But we are only guessing on this, because to our knowledge no one has ever researched the relationship between infant temperament and faith in adulthood. What does seem clear from the research is that parents can influence the degree to which a baby will grow up to trust other people and perhaps even God. Trust is needed to have faith, and thus the child who is very trusting may be more likely to have a strong faith in God (or perhaps equally likely to have faith in other people or self).[5]

Faith Builds upon Trust

What can parents do to influence a baby to become trusting and thus to have faith? A trustworthy, predictable environment is important. When parents and other caretakers quickly provide for the child's needs, and the environment is stable and marked by regular routines, the baby is

---

5. This idea is most clearly emphasized in the research and theory of Erik Erikson in *Childhood and Society*.

more likely to be trusting. A chaotic environment where the baby's needs and cries are often ignored is likely to produce a child that is distrustful of the environment.[6]

Thus the best thing a parent can do to have a trusting baby is to regularly care for the infant's needs and work hard to have a relatively predictable home life. Furthermore, if the baby is cared for outside the home on a regular basis, the caretakers should do the same—give regular needed care in a fairly calm and predictable environment. Likewise the church should provide the same for the child. Youngsters need loving attention and care wherever they are. The likely result tends to be a trusting child and later a trusting adult, who is more likely to have faith.

Now one can make a case that a very trusting child should not be the ultimate goal. Children need to learn to trust some people, but not to trust everyone. Youngsters should have strong faith in God, but not as much faith in other people or perhaps even in themselves. A strong trust and faith in God is certainly desirable, and usually it is desirable for the child to be trusting of the parent. But others do not deserve and should not receive the child's trust, such as bullies and unknown strangers. We don't want our children to have faith in false religions. Should parents not be so predictable and responsive to their children?

Both outer and internal factors will limit the amount of trust a child develops. First, parents and other caretakers are physically unable to meet the child's every desire and need. There are times when the parent must continue to drive the car in spite of the baby's wanting some milk. Likewise if the parent or caretaker has other children who need care, the baby may have to wait a few minutes before having the diaper changed. Often parents have a difficult time reading the baby's cues as to what is needed. Thus, realistically, it is probably impossible to spoil a baby, at least during the first year of life.

There is also an inward limitation on trust development. Beginning about six months of age for most babies, and then increasing and continuing for a year or more, children tend to become attached to the most available caretakers, whether parents, babysitters, or others who care for the baby. They prefer that person or to those persons to whom they are most securely attached.[7] Thus the child as a part of normal development

6. Again see Erikson, *Childhood and Society.*

7. It should be noted that some babies do not become securely attached to one or more adults. These children may overreact to separation, or in contrast be ambivalent to par-

even in the most positive environment will naturally be more trusting of some people than others. The key person for building trust is whoever regularly provides for the baby's needs. Thus the child learns to have faith in some people and not in others.

Of course, faith is more than just trusting, but faith does build upon trust. Faith will also be influenced by the parents' and other people's teaching later in the preschool and school years. Faith will also be influenced by what the young child and school-age child sees in the parents; if a parent has strong faith in God, and the child sees positive results of that faith, the child is more likely to imitate that faith. The faith of other adults, including teachers at school and in church, can also influence the child's degree of faith and the object (God, other people, or self) in which he or she has faith. When the child expresses faith in God, and God is seen as trustworthy and deserving of faith, then the faith is likely to grow. The parent and other adults in the children's environment can influence this perception by regularly talking about how God provides and cares for the child. Discussing God's influence with your children becomes more important as they move through the preschool and school years. We suspect that sensitivity to God's work is a key reason why the Bible encourages infusion of God's principles in everyday life.

Feelings about God

Infants are unlikely to have a clear concept of God. Such an understanding begins to develop at about the time the child starts talking, but for some time the concept of God is likely to be confused with the concept of the parent. During the late preschool and early school years, the concept of parent and the concept of God become more distinct, but even in adulthood some of the remnants of this confusion remain: We often tend to have feelings about God that are like our feelings about one or both of our parents. Feelings and emotions are important aspects of the infant's life. Children and adults are unlikely to recall events before age two, because these kinds of memories require verbal abilities (the ability to talk and understand what others say). But feelings about the world, about parents, and even about words are very important during infancy.

---

ents and other caretakers. Paul Meier and I consider some of the research on attachment in our *Raising Your Child*, as do Stanley Fitch and I in *Insights into Child Development*. This topic is also considered in almost every child-development textbook.

How can a parent influence such feelings? Again, a loving environment where there is interaction and physical contact is important.[8] We must never forget that Jesus took infants and children into his arms (Mark 10:16). Caressing and holding the child gently but firmly communicates emotional warmth and caring. We have amazed some parents of very young infants when we can sometimes stop a baby's crying by simply holding a bit more firmly than the parent had been. Of course it is possible to overdo this, and some babies cannot be comforted so easily because they have a difficult temperament, or because they have needs other than touch at the moment.

As you hold your baby and give needed attention, talk to her, sing to her, and include some words related to God. The baby will not understand what the words mean, but you will be building positive emotional associations between the sounds of the words and the loving care you are providing. Saying or singing the words gently, as the child enjoys the comfort of being held or touched, will link the God-related words to positive emotions. Later the child will come to understand the meaning of the words, but even during infancy youngsters come to like some words more than others because of such associations. On the other hand, if words related to God and the Christian faith are associated with anger, deprivation, or neglect, the later emotional reaction to them may be negative. Why is it that some infants become children (and adults) who are attracted to the church and to God, and that for others the reaction to the spiritual is just the opposite? The emotional reactions may possibly be traced to infancy, although later experiences can also influence the emotional associations that develop. But too often parents and churches focus on the meaning of words and forget the emotional tone of words, and the emotional associations the words may have for an individual.

Similarly, emotions may become associated with certain people, locations, and things in the environment. It may be that children are attracted to the physical characteristics of a Bible (the smell and feel of a leather-covered Bible), a church building, or even a pastor, because positive associations may be traced to childhood or even infancy. These may be repulsive for other children because pain or discomfort have long been associated with them. I (Don) once had a teacher who disliked

---

8. Ashley Montagu wrote a very important book that has now gone through three editions, titled *Touching*, in which he documents from thousands of research studies how important touch is to both human and animal development. Both physical and emotional development are influenced by touch.

most anything religious because he had teachers in a parochial school who had slapped his hands regularly with a ruler. It was hard to talk with him about God and faith, not because of his misunderstandings of these topics, but because of the emotional pain with which they were associated.

The Spiritual Experiences of Infants

Do babies have spiritual experiences? Do they experience God? At first thought, this seems unlikely. Infants do not have the degree of brain development that older children have, and their intellectual capacity is limited to nonverbal associations: the tone of words, emotional associations, and thinking that does not depend on understanding language.

Yet a number of researchers make a case that infants develop rather vague impressions that eventually become a concept of God.[9] While this may seem doubtful, the fact that reported spiritual experiences of children tend to become less frequent with age (because of negative reactions from peers and some adults) could suggest that babies have frequent spiritual experiences during the infant years.

Consider, for example, a baby who discovers her hand for the first time. She will probably put part or even all of her hand in her mouth, exploring by touch and taste what it is like. Then she is likely to take it out and examine it carefully with her eyes. She will be fascinated with this object that was always there but that only now is she really seeing and exploring.

In such a situation, it seems obvious that the baby is filled with awe and wonder as she is exploring the hand. Her never having seen or explored this part of the world before, this must be an overwhelming experience that, at least in the secular sense of the term, can be considered *spiritual*. With so many new objects and people for the infant to explore, perhaps the months of infancy are filled with spiritual experiences. Even

9. I surveyed many of these research studies in an article titled "Baby Faith," 117–26. Technically speaking, the researchers suggest that infants are prepared for the faith community and develop the precursor to the God concept, termed the "numinous" or "ultimate background object" from the simple interactions and games that adults play with babies. Of course these researchers are not able to interview infants to be sure of these assumptions, and many of their conclusions are generalizations of research about other aspects of infancy or extrapolating (extending backward) theories based upon the study of preschoolers.

being cuddled and stroked must be wonderful to the baby. Keep in mind that the definition of this kind of spiritual experience can include despair as well as delight. Thus there may be a similar degree of spiritual intensity when the infant is hungry, has a dirty diaper, experiences pain or fear, or is sleepy. Thus it is at least possible that spiritual experiences are frequent during infancy, although it is also possible that there are times when the baby is not having a spiritual experience.

If the infant does have such experiences, is God involved? Here we must be very cautious. We do not know. However, the Bible does speak of praise coming from the "lips of . . . infants" (Ps 8:2). We are told that the Hebrew for the English word *infant* translates literally as "suckling baby": an infant who is not yet weaned from the breast.[10] Actually this does not indicate a particular age, given that some sources suggest that children during ancient times might continue to occasionally breastfeed until age three or four.[11] Allowing for the possibility that this could be a poetic description rather than literal praise coming from babies, a mystical connection between God and the infant is somehow possible, a connection not to be confused with salvation.[12] If such a mystical connection can occur, then we have in the infant's experience an example of common grace, grace that comes from God prior to salvation. It may be that the baby's awe and wonder at the world, and then the infant's connecting events, experiencing repetitious movements, and imitating the environment may produce delight. Thus the praise described in Psalm 8 may be expressed in the baby's mind in a manner only seen by God, while we see it reflected facial expressions and body movements. We may also hear auditory praise such as cooing, laughing, and, later, babbling.

If this is the case, then when the child develops a conscience, and the sin nature is expressed in sinful behavior and sinful thinking, that is the point of departure from this connection with God. "I want" and "I will" increasingly displace the awe and wonder. The latent sin nature now comes front and center. Perhaps we all are to become, then, examples of the prodigal son about whom Jesus spoke, by disconnecting from

10. Personal conversation with Dr. Joseph Sprinkle, a professor of Hebrew and a Bible translator.

11. White, "Family," 498.

12. Some denominations suggest that infant baptism is associated with either entering into the church community or receiving the Holy Spirit. Yet most such churches also have additional rites that represent a deeper level of commitment to God and the church, usually during the school years or in the preteen years.

God through sin, and then potentially coming back to God in salvation through the forgiveness of sin. But this coming back is more than just returning to a mere connection to God; now we are in a genuine and potentially maturing relationship with God, and even are adopted as sons and daughters of God: "co-heirs with Christ" as the Scripture teaches (Rom 8:17).

Discussing the spiritual experiences of babies is ultimately a speculative matter, and we must hedge a bit about our conclusions. On one hand, perhaps we see what we expect to see in infants. On the other hand, we must be careful not to limit God. He may be wonderfully at work in a baby's life, and it may be that his involvement makes the child and later the adult long for something once had but now missing. That longing may indeed be the void that—as Pascal said—only God can fill. Perhaps it is a longing to once again be in the arms of Christ, to experience the world and our Creator with all the vibrancy of a baby who has never seen such things before.

Babies as Examples

Babies can teach much to us parents, as well as to other adults. For example, the Bible uses the analogy of birth to represent how people become part of the kingdom of God through salvation. One thinks of the tiny fertilized cell at conception as something like the initial stages of interest in the Christian faith. (To describe the beginnings of the kingdom of God, Jesus also uses the metaphor of planting seeds, which is also parallel to conception.) We have also been impressed at how women are like God in that they are willing to sacrifice their lives, or nearly so, during childbirth, in order that a new life can be born. The parallel between the mother and God is very biblical (Isa 66:13; Matt 23.37).

We are impressed with Christ's comment, "I tell you the truth, anyone who will not receive the kingdom of God like a little child will never enter it," and the phrase in the preceding verse that says "the kingdom of God belongs to such as these [children]" (Mark 10:14–15). As in Psalm 8:2, alluded to earlier, this mention of children most clearly relates to suckling babies, and thus provides a vivid picture of our relationship with God, that is like the mother breastfeeding the baby. We would like to explore this metaphor to see how the infant at the mother's breast is like the believer interacting with God.

We are impressed with the total dependence as well as beauty of a child at the breast. Babies would be unlikely to survive all by themselves, even surrounded by a smorgasbord of food. They need to be supported, encouraged, and given individual attention. God interacts with us in a distinctive manner. Individualizing the spiritual instruction of our children should also take into account particular interests and limitations as well, and we should seek out a church context that provides individual attention for our youngsters.

While at the mother's breast, a baby experiences intimacy with the mother because of the close physical contact, just as God is close to us, even within us. A child is cradled in the mother's arms, even as we experience the touch of God on our lives. Mother and child smile at and delight in each other, even as we can be delighted by God and seek his pleasure and delight in us. The quiet, soothing voice of the mother reminds us of God's still, small voice as he cares for us. Babies sometimes gurgle with delight while feeding, and some milk may be spilled in the process. We as Christians can live rather messy lives as well, yet we continue to sense God's presence and care as he cleans us. An older baby might even babble a bit during a meal, and likewise the words in our praise to God may not be as important as what is bubbling within us. The baby drinks to survive, even as we drink of God's spiritual milk of the Word. The liquid keeps the baby from dehydrating, and we too realize that spiritual dryness will take away life and vitality. The baby drinks in spurts, and similarly we cannot take in all of God's word at one time. The baby sucks, tastes, and swallows; we receive God's word, reflect upon it, and apply it to our lives. Early in infancy the baby's eyes produce the clearest picture at the precise distance between the baby's head and the mother's face when breast-feeding. Similarly, we need to be focused on God and keep distractions out of focus and, if possible, out of view. Thus we see an overwhelming picture of our spiritual lives in the baby's feeding from the mother's breast.

As the baby is held by the mother (feeding or not), an intriguing pattern is going on that prepares the child for conversation during childhood and adulthood. This interaction sequence involves the mother's talking to the baby as if the baby were responding to her. She will ask a question, pause, and then respond to the baby as if something has been said in return. A few weeks later, or perhaps even sooner, the child will make a vocal noise of some kind. The mother will express great interest and again will act as if the noise is a response to her. She may even pick up cues (such as an indication of hunger) from the baby's actions and respond with food, just as if the baby had verbally told her of the hunger. With time and repetition, the baby makes more specific vocalizations, and eventually the "as-if" sequence becomes real interaction, with both mother and child talking to each other.

In a somewhat similar way, Jesus told his disciples—and others in his audience—things that puzzled them, yet he acted as if they would understand. They remembered such comments, studied them, and with the Holy Spirit's help came to understand them. Initially they were confused, but Jesus's acting "as if" they understood encouraged them to work at that understanding. Elsewhere the Bible says, "Be holy in all you do; for it is written: 'Be holy, because I am holy'" (1 Pet 1:15–16). To be as perfect and sinless as God is an overwhelming expectation, but perhaps God treats us as if we are holy so that we move toward that ideal. God expects us to become more like him, to move towards his character, and perhaps this is what he sees in us "as if" it were actually the case. Two great sociologists once commented, "If men define situations as real, they are real in their consequences."[13]

God acts "as if" we are spiritually competent. Sometimes we may say, "God, I'm not really there yet; I'm not ready for this yet." Perhaps we are not, but he acts as if we are, because he knows that will help move us in the right direction. Does God not see what we are really like? Of course he does, just as the mother realizes the infant is not really interacting . . . yet. But the "as-if" approach motivates and encourages us to move in the direction of spiritual competence.

This is a good example for us as parents. Perhaps if we will act and talk as if our children are growing in their spiritual lives, this will encourage growth. That is not to say it is easy, especially when their incompetence is glaring. It is not lying to realize what our children can be, and will become if they choose to. Perhaps they will make that choice to grow if we communicate the expectation "as if" they were already growing.

---

13. Thomas and Thomas, *The Child in America*, 572.

THREE

Crawling, Walking, and Running toward God

Toddlers and Preschoolers

Deb was near exasperation. Her two-year-old daughter was once again banging on the door to go outside and play even though Deb had told her she could do so after she had her nap. But lying down to sleep just was not in her daughter's list of things to do. "No nap—go out," the youngster insisted in no uncertain tone of voice. She continued to push on the door, as she had done for the last twenty minutes. Deb was now torn—she had drawn the line, and her daughter obviously was ignoring it. Should she spank her daughter because of her willful ignoring of her mother's command? To do so would teach her daughter the justice of God. But was her little girl really in rebellion against authority—or did she just have her own mind? Perhaps to take her back to the bedroom—again—would be another lesson in the mercy of God. But Deb was certain this could not go on forever. She felt she had come to the end of her patience.

WHILE BABIES CAN TEACH us some things about God, and the foundations of faith, including faith in God, are made during infancy, it is in the toddler years and especially the preschool period that children actually learn something about God and spirituality from parents. The goal during these years is not just to look to the distant future of relative spiritual maturity but rather to prize the little people they already are and encourage these youngsters to learn about God and understand their spiritual experiences. For the spiritually precocious preschooler, there may even be an experience of salvation, although this becomes more likely in school-aged children.

Teddy Bears and God

As noted in the previous chapter, babies usually become very attached to one or both parents, and occasionally to a caretaker if he or she takes care of the child more than do other adults. When things go well with the child and the one or more adults who regularly care for the child, then there tends to be a strong attachment. Thus the child may cry when an individual leaves, a common problem in Sunday school classes especially among children who are one and two years old. (Sometimes this can occur with three-year-olds as well.) Usually within a few minutes, the child will become involved with other children and the Sunday school teacher, if encouraged to do so and if the class is interesting. Of course if the child is not feeling well, the crying may continue. It is very important that church staff and volunteers accurately read why the child is crying and respond appropriately.[1]

Note that we said, "when things go well" in the last paragraph. Sometimes things do not go well. It may be that the parent has not developed a strong relationship with the child or has not been as dependable as necessary, and thus the child may not be strongly attached. Instead of crying when the parent leaves, the child may just withdraw or have prolonged crying upon the parent's departure. Sometimes when the parent returns to pick up the child, the less attached child will not be interested in going or may be upset with the parent. What is important to note is that good or poor attachment is not entirely the parent's doing. Sometimes the child's inborn temperament is more of an influence upon attachment than is the way the parent acts toward the child. Children that are high in negative emotions and low in social characteristics are especially likely to have weak attachment, even if the parent has done her best to connect with the child. We simply cannot always blame the

1. It is also important for parents to carefully consider their child's reaction to the nursery or other church context. One of our children had a very strong aversion to attending junior church—even starting to cry when we approached the outside of the church. Upon further inspection, we discovered that several older children were "assistants" who bullied the little children regularly and painfully. When the staff said there was nothing they could do because the older kids were "an elder's sons," we quickly decided to change churches.

parents for the degree of attachment that develops; the child may have been born a difficult child, and the parent can only do her best to give attention and love in the moments the child is willing. Again, reading the child's cues is what is most important.[2]

Attachment produces a "separation anxiety" that produces the crying and other negative behavior when the parent leaves. However, youngsters between age one and three also want to explore the environment. Thus it is not unusual to see children move between wanting the parent's assurance and encouragement and then wanting to be independent and do it on their own. This can shift back and forth within just a few minutes of time. If possible, it is often best for the parent to be flexible—encouraging when the child comes running, but also able to discipline when the child insists on disobeying. It is not always easy to know whether the child deserves discipline for refusing to do things the parent's way, or whether the child has simply forgotten what is required.[3]

As a child vacillates between wanting comfort and reassurance and then desiring independence and self-sufficiency, the child often becomes attached to an object that (at least temporarily) serves as a substitute attachment figure. Often this object is a blanket, a favorite teddy bear, or some other object. (My—Don's—mother told me I had a favorite baby bottle that I took everywhere, and I'm still very attached to food!) It is by having this substitute for the parent that the child can boldly venture out on her own without the parent by her side.[4]

2. As noted in the previous chapter, attachment is usually a major topic in any child-development text. Note that, for the sake of readability, we are combining several different kinds of attachment under the labels "poor," "weak," and the like. This follows the traditional view that anything apart from strong attachment is less than healthy. However, I depart from the traditional view in suggesting that attachment is not just the parent's doing, which is consistent with recent research on the topic. It should be noted that children can also attach to the peer group. This kind of attachment takes place in communal groups and, for homeless children who must depend upon peers for survival, in street gangs.

3. Dobson, *Dare to Discipline*, makes the distinction between willful behavior (deserving punishment) and childish behavior (deserving correction). While we like the distinction and the alternative responses he suggests, we often had a difficult time telling when a child was rebelling or being thoughtless.

4. Here we are describing what is usually called "object-relations theory." The substitute for the attached parent is technically called a "transitional object." See Winnicott, *Playing and Reality*. A good book that deals with this topic and how it relates to the development of the concept of God is Rizzuto's *The Birth of the Living God*. Interestingly,

We will never forget when one of our sons—at about age two or three—accidentally left his favorite bear at a distant church we had visited. He suddenly realized his loss many miles from the church and burst into tears. His softhearted father and mother turned the car around and retraced those miles to bring comfort to their beloved son. Neither of us will ever forget the gigantic smile that came to a little boy's face when he was finally reunited with his favorite stuffed animal!

As the months go by, the substitute object usually becomes less and less important until the school years when most children leave this object at home. This does not mean that the teddy bear or blanket is no longer important; indeed I have found that even some of my (Don's) university students tell me they still have the old teddy bear and keep it in their dorm room! But I'm sure the purpose of the object is no longer security and separation from the parent.

All of this about attachment and attachment objects is important because evidence shows that this process of becoming attached relates to the development of the child's concept of God. Without the presence of the parent, an object replaces the parent as a means of security. The growing child comes to realize that he or she can still be safe and secure without the object. What is it that protects when neither the parent nor the object is at hand? Many children come to believe it must be God. This belief, of course, is often encouraged by adults who teach the child to pray for safety, and who talk about God's protection and love for the child. This sense of God's being present and keeping the child safe may grow out of earlier spiritual experiences in infancy, as described in the last chapter. The child may continue to have experiences of awe and wonder from time to time, but very often such experiences include the attachment object close at hand. With time, the idea of God takes the place of the object. Interestingly, researchers have found that even in families where the child is not taught about God, the child still develops the concept of God, although the view of God tends to be more frightening and gloomy.[5]

---

a number of Christian graduate schools of psychology emphasize this theory, and some of the best research studies related to it are produced by doctoral students at these schools.

5. This is mentioned in an extensive review of the research on concepts of God among preschoolers, from which some of this chapter is drawn. Tamminen, et al., "The Religious Concepts of Preschoolers," 59–81.

Parents: The Child's First God?

If the concept of God does indeed emerge from the attachment object that takes the place of the parent/s, it makes sense that the concept of God would be somewhat similar to parents. After all, the object replaced the parents, and now God replaces the object. Research of children's concepts of God in general affirms the powerful similarity between a child's view of parents and of God—sometimes favoring the mother, sometimes the father, but most often combining the mother and father's characteristics.

The connection between the child's view of God and parents is also encouraged by addressing God as the Father, as Jesus and others in the Bible did, and as we still do today. This can produce problems for those whose fathers have neglected or abused them. Even as adults, it is very easy to unconsciously think of God as being like one parent or the other. Sometimes adults must receive counseling to overcome this tendency to see negative parental characteristics in God.

Certainly one moral to this is that parents need to be the best representation of God that they can to their preschool children. To realize that at the emotional level, feelings about one or both parents are likely to become the feelings the child will have about God should bring us parents to our knees as we attempt to be as loving and caring as God.

The child's view of God during these years is often very much like the child's view of a human being. Thus the humanity of Jesus is likely to be understood quite clearly. He may be seen as a good friend and protector. When asked to draw God, often children of Christian parents will draw a picture of a man and say it is a picture of Jesus. However, the divinity of Christ is submerged if not absent. God and Jesus are considered to be synonymous, as children are unlikely to have any concept of the Trinity. (Indeed, understanding the Trinity is difficult even for theologians who have spent a lifetime trying to understand this idea!) At best, Jesus may be seen as a more or less super-man, not unlike the hero Superman himself.

Is it worth trying to teach a preschooler that God is more than a man with some extraordinary powers? To belabor this truth will probably be fruitless and frustrating to both you and your preschooler. However, you can introduce from time to time comments discrepant from the child's view of God. For example, you might comment that God made the whole world, and yet made it out of nothing. This will probably bewilder the child, but that is probably a good thing. God should bewilder us, as that is part of his nature. God is much greater than we are. There are times, for example, to tell your child, "No one knows everything about God. He is very mysterious. Isn't it amazing that he can love us, and yet we don't understand everything about him?" It is better for the child to sense the mystery surrounding God than for ideas about God to be simplified to the point that they are misleading. A good rule of thumb for teaching a preschooler about God is never to teach something about God that will need to be reversed in the future. Too many adolescents and adults think they have rejected God, when they have rejected only a childish, simplistic notion of God that lacks mystery, ultimate power, incredible wisdom, and other aspects of "otherness."[6]

But what of the situation where one of the parents is missing from the home, or where both parents are present but one is far from being like God in attitudes and character? It will be easy for the child to see God as harsh and oppressive if a parent is abusive. If this is an ongoing problem, and the parent is not repentant (or merely acts repentant but continues the behavior), one can make a case for marital separation— if not for the other parent's then for the children's sake. Neglect and abuse are always evil, but when present in a parent these behaviors not only affect the child personally but also affect the child's spiritual life. Indulgence (the other extreme) is not quite as bad as abuse or neglect, if one parent's discipline can offset the indulgence of the other. If both parents are indulgent, however, God may be viewed as lacking justice, and as unconcerned about sin. It seems likely that some children reject God because they see God as being like one parent or the other, who falls far short of being like God.

If the child must see a neglectful or abusive parent because of visitation rights, it is imperative for the custodial parent to minimize the stress involved, and to try to distinguish God from that parent. For example, a mother might tell a child, "God is much better than any parent can be. Sometimes Mommy or Daddy can do wrong things, but God never does anything wrong. He's better than anyone in the whole world." Of course

6. I am sure one could overdo this emphasis as well, but adults usually tend to err on the side of oversimplifying the concept of God. A "bite-size" view of God is misleading and does not fit the real world. Listen to Nichole Nordeman's song "Who You Are" for an example of this problem.

advice and instruction by the parent may not be sufficient; in some cases of abuse and neglect, the child (or adult survivor) will need counseling to reveal underlying problems and to clearly separate the experience with the poor parent from the view of God, both in the child's thinking and emotions.

Experiences of God and Angels in the Preschool Years

Do preschoolers experience God and angelic beings? While we cannot be absolutely certain, the occasional reports of children seeing angels or God should not be automatically rejected. Given that children have emerged from infancy, which is thought to be characterized by numerous spiritual experiences of awe and wonder, it should not surprise us if such experiences continue to occur, although less frequently. If these experiences involve the realm of the spirit, then it would make sense for at least some young children to encounter beings from that realm. It could be that some children have an unusual degree of sensitivity to the spirit realm and thus are more receptive to such experiences. But we must admit this has not been established by careful research.

What is perhaps more common are children's fears of the dark, of dogs, and of other things. These fears might be explained by suggesting that disturbing events have been linked with such things. (A dog's biting or jumping up on a child might produce a fear of dogs, for instance.[7]) But learning fears by association does not adequately explain the origin of all such fears. Perhaps children intuitively sense that evil in this world is linked to fallen angels in the spirit realm. Thus there is potential for threats in the darkness of this sense world, which may bring the spirit realm to the forefront.

I recall my (Don's) own fears of the dark when I was not much older than a preschooler. I was convinced someone lived in the attic of our ancient house, and that the only opening to the attic was in the closet of my bedroom. Not once could I sleep in the room because of the fear. I felt safer in my father's room because he had Bible storybooks that he read to me each evening. Those books, and my father, kept me safe from

---

7. This kind of learning is called "classical conditioning," the result of paired associations, contrasted with "operant conditioning," which refers to learning as the result of reinforcement.

the evil thing I was convinced was in the attic. Considering the total lack of evidence of anyone ever going to that attic, perhaps I intuitively realized that the attic was like another realm, a realm that included Satan and his evil angels.

I also recall our own children having such fears and the illogical basis for such fears. There was no learning experience that would adequately account for the fear of the dark that all our children had at one time or another during their early years. Perceptions may also differ by age. Once when one of our boys was a preschooler, I climbed a ladder and pushed my way through an opening in the ceiling to do some work in the attic. As soon as I had disappeared from view, my son ran through the house screaming, "The house ate Daddy!"

One time when our children and some friends were arguing over who would get the most money from selling some of their possessions, they argued heatedly, then stopped suddenly as they sensed something terrible was happening in the spirit realm. They immediately began praying about a number of things, including the family car. They laid hands on one another as they prayed for their friends and family. Then they felt the evil lift, and the demonic influence was gone. They had sensed the darkness but also experienced its leaving because of their prayers. They saw all of this with spiritual eyes, not physical eyes. Now some might rack this up to fabrication on their part, but our children rarely told untruths, and when someone would, another of our children would gladly tell. In this case they all consistently told the same story, even when we talked with them individually. Some might say they had vivid imaginations, but again we only recall this happening once. Could it be that they were more sensitive to the spirit realm, and indeed that an evil presence had been removed because of their prayers?

On other occasions they would tell us of their fears of something evil present, usually at bedtime. We would then pray with them and ask God to remove anything evil. This brought comfort to them most of the time. Thus when the children sensed evil in broad daylight after the above-mentioned argument occurred, they simply followed our example. Again, we cannot absolutely prove that the spirit realm was involved in these events, but we believe it is possible. To dismiss such experiences as imagination may inadvertently teach your kids that you do not believe in Satan or his angels, and perhaps even call into question whether there is actually a God. Perhaps the "boogey man" and other fears are a psychological projection of a latent realization that Satan and other evil beings really exist in the spirit realm.

Parents need to teach their children how to combat evil in the spirit realm, even if it is possible that they are fighting only vivid imaginations. God knows the source of the struggle, and we believe he answers the prayers of a young child (or of an adult, for that matter). Regardless, we encourage you to take seriously plausible reports of evil in the spirit realm but not add to children's anxiety by dwelling on the problem. Similarly, it probably is best not to emphasize their supposed encounters with God or his angels, but also do not be quick to dismiss them. It may be best to take such reports as a matter of fact—unless there is clear reason to doubt the report. Pray with the child if need be, but take it all with a grain of salt. Often it helps to tell children that their friend Jesus is stronger than any evil thing, and he is with them all the time, wherever they are, which is actually the first step to understanding the omnipresence of God (God's being everywhere at all times).

Share Your Faith and Track Your Child's Faith

One of the themes of this book is that you and your child need to share in spiritual growth and experience. One way to accomplish this is to tell your children the faith stories and aspects of the ongoing journey that has shaped your spiritual life. They need to hear something of your struggles and victories. You might describe to them your own conversion experience and some of the things you have learned about faith that they can understand. If they come to perceive that you gradually grew in your faith, it will be an encouragement to them to know they are not expected to be where you are immediately. We also encourage you to share the story of their birth, and of other key moments in their lives, and how God was at work through those experiences. Share with them how you prayed for them, and how God answered those prayers.

While stories of the past are important, and children often want to hear stories about themselves repeated again and again, you should also share with them what God is doing with you at present, assuming they can comprehend something of what you are talking about and if it is appropriate for children. A preschooler may not fully understand your account of what God is doing in your life at present, but the child can understand that God is working with you, and therefore God is real and important to you. Children should receive that message in many ways on a regular basis, as it not only affirms the reality of your relationship with God but also serves as a model for them to imitate.

Speak to them of the neighbor or relative for whom you are praying and to whom you are witnessing. Encourage your children to pray for these folks as well. Now perhaps it might be somewhat embarrassing if your preschooler then tells the neighbor or relative about your prayers for them. But that report from your naïve preschooler may be what could break down some resistance. The innocence of a small child may make the report compelling to that loved one who needs the Lord. A bit of embarrassment may be worth the result. But of course be sure you are being led of the Lord when you share such things with your child.

Encourage your child to talk with you as well about his or her feelings and experiences related to God. Sometimes well-meaning parents have one-direction teaching, telling their children what they should know without providing some time for response. If your children begin telling you about their joys or struggles, encourage them by listening, by asking questions, and accepting what they say. Sometimes having your child draw pictures for you can help her reveal her thoughts and feelings about God, church, and other religious issues. Ask the child to draw a picture about God or some aspect of faith, then have the youngster explain the drawing. Sometimes things that are difficult for a preschooler—or even school-aged child—to put into words can be reflected in drawings, and then the child can better put the ideas into words as they reflect on the drawings.[8]

Make a notebook of your child's spiritual development, recording what he or she tells you and including prayer requests that concern your child. Occasionally review some of the notebook, especially when a prayer is answered, or when some new development reflects growth from previous notations. Keeping such a notebook communicates that the spiritual life is important, even worthy of a parent's keeping a special

8. Robert Coles used this method in his famous research study called *The Spiritual Life of Children*. The method is even more clearly illustrated in a DVD produced by the Public Broadcasting Service (PBS) titled *Listening to Children: A Moral Journey with Robert Coles*, which includes interviews with children. Youngsters describe spiritual aspects of drawings. The program is a good teaching tool for parents who want to use this method, and when your child moves into the school years, parents might invite them to watch the video together, further emphasizing to the importance of spirituality and faith.

book about their experiences and growth. While daily notations would be great, including both things that the child wants recorded as well as some of your own notes, nearly any parent can make at least a paragraph notation about a child's spiritual development once a week. If you absolutely cannot keep such a journal (which is also a good way to document your own spiritual journey), then consider keeping a verbal record on an audio recorder. As the child moves into the school-age years, the notebook or recording will continue to record the development of the child's faith journey. Someday, when your child is an adult, you may want to copy it for them.

Guidelines for Teaching Your Preschooler

We would like to share with you some suggestions for teaching your youngster. Keep in mind, however, that you probably know your child better than anyone, and thus you are likely to know which of these guidelines is most important. Watch the results of your teaching, both in your child's speech and actions, as these are important indications of whether your teaching is effective. Again, don't try to teach a lot of content at one time; two to five minutes of instruction every day or two is much better than thirty minutes once a week. Keep applications short and focused; preschoolers probably won't be able to apply stories to their own lives, so you will have to help them do so. Be sure to pick up on the child's cues as to when they have had enough teaching, or when you need to change your approach. "Mom, can we do something else?" is a clear indication that you should do just that.

Involve the child actively, using drama, drawing, puppets, dance, and other methods (see chapter 6). Use as many of the senses as possible, including sound, smell, touch, and sight. Movement often helps a child become involved in the story or lesson, unless of course you are telling a Bible story at the end of the day and part of your goal is to help your child go to sleep!

Speaking of Bible stories at night, many parents find bedtime to be the ideal time to talk with the child. The day's events are likely to be on the child's mind, and the parent's review of the day may help the child see the spiritual dimension of what has taken place. A Bible story and prayer can complete the time together. The major advantage of such an evening devotional is that it becomes a reward of sorts if it is presented as the only way the child can stay up for a few minutes past the official bedtime.

When telling stories, use books with lots of pictures that do not look ancient. Use inflection in your voice, and let your expressiveness affect your face. You may find that your preschooler wants to hear the same story seemingly a hundred times. The familiar can be comforting to the child, as is doing the same thing at the same time each evening. It gives order and continuity to a life that may seem chaotic to the child. Remember, you have been through life for many more years, so what seems mundane to you may be not be so for the child, and thus the child may welcome the familiar and predictable. Repeating stories may even encourage spiritual experience, just as it does for some of us who may have heard the Christmas story, the song "Amazing Grace," or even a favorite compact disk a dozen times, yet we are moved in spite of—or due to—the familiarity.

Here is a word of warning about Bible storybooks for children. Not all storybooks are well written. Furthermore, not all stories are told accurately. If you are not very familiar with the Bible, you might read over the relevant passages before using a storybook for kids. When our children were in their preschool and early elementary years, I (Don) began reading the story of Noah to them. When the animals and people were all in the ark, the storybook said, Noah closed the door. This detail just didn't sound right, so I finished the story and then got my Bible out. I told them what the Bible said (specifically that God, not Noah, had closed the door of the ark [Gen 7:16]) and pointed out that we have to be careful, because not everything that people say is in the Bible really is there. I think it was a good lesson for them to learn that books are not always perfect, even books about the Bible.

Many children use formula prayers during the preschool and early elementary years. "Now I lay me down to sleep" is perhaps the most popular formula prayer. We don't think there is anything wrong with formula prayers if the child is not just saying the words to get them finished. If you don't provide a formula prayer, your child may make one up, such as the one often invented by small children: "God bless mommy and daddy and my sister and my brother, etc. Amen." However, you might encourage the child from time to time to include some of the specific requests that you had talked about before the prayer, and to really tell God anything they want to say. Some children never use formula prayers, but even when we encouraged our children to say what was really on their hearts, they would pray a formula prayer. Our daughter's favorite was, "Lord, keep me safe this very night, and quiet all my fears. / Bless and guard me while I sleep, till morning light appears."

Whenever you teach your child, keep things interactive. Avoid lectures, which are easy to tune out. Instead listen for where the child is and talk within that framework. Ideally, discussion of an issue comes during a "teachable moment" when a child asks a question; this will connect better than your imposing something out of the blue. Infuse the Bible into things you do together, be that riding in the car, pulling weeds in the garden, or watching a TV show. (We are convinced commercials are made for the mute button so that spiritual discussions can occur between parent and child.)

When your child makes a comment that includes some theological or technical inaccuracy, be careful not to overreact. You can affirm the sharing as you correct the youngster. For instance, a parent might say, "Yes, Jesus is really strong and does wonderful things, even if he isn't Superman." Never make your teaching unpleasant, and of you see your child becoming bored with what you are teaching, either end quickly or change your method.[9]

What should you teach? Usually the simpler Bible storybooks appropriate for preschoolers have already chosen the key stories they can understand, and omitted biblical passages that deal with graphic violence, which might produce nightmares. But it is good to check before buying. Children tend to love the story of creation, perhaps because they have created drawings and other things, so they can identify with the story. We recall one of our children delightedly pointing out things that God had made, including some in which God's direct creation was debatable (such as electric wires)! We taught our children, as well as preschoolers at church and at a preschool where Brenda worked, the Ten Commandments. Some of them had to be adapted.

One subject that we think you should not emphasize, although you might mention it, is salvation. Some preschoolers are ready to become Christians, but to pressure children who are uncertain or who only vaguely understand is to be insensitive to where they are spiritually. I

9. This is a key principle with children of any age—but particularly with preschoolers since you are setting the tone for their attitudes about spiritual matters perhaps for the rest of their lives.

(Don) became a Christian in a church service when I was six years old, and each of our children came to the Lord between four and six years of age. But we only told them about salvation when they asked about it, or when they seemed ready for it. (We will consider aspects of leading your child to the Lord in chapter 5.)

The overall message of your teaching for preschoolers should be that God loves them and protects them. We believe they need to hear about God's judgment and justice during the school years, but hopefully the first thing youngsters hear about God is that he loves and cares for them. Jesus usually spoke to the nonreligious person with compassion and forgiveness, not judgment.

Encouraging the Preschooler's Experience of God

Can parents encourage their children to have spiritual experiences, even direct experiences of God? As noted in an earlier chapter, one cannot dictate to God when and where you will experience him. If this were possible, then God would no longer be the sovereign God that he is, for we would be in control. However, we can make ourselves and our children accessible to God, and thus if he so chooses, we will be prepared to receive the experience God desires.

Catherine Stonehouse, a seminary teacher, has adapted a method called Godly Play in a variety of evangelical denominations.[10] Her work as well as the work of the originator, Jerome Berryman, indicates that children often have spiritual experiences with God when the Godly Play

---

10. Berryman's landmark book on the topic is titled *Godly Play*, although he has also written or helped write several manuals that are more curriculum based. Generally his approach is designed for church contexts that are liturgical. Jerome is an Episcopalian priest who comes from a Presbyterian background; he taught and worked with dying and seriously ill children at a Baptist medical school in Houston. He draws some of his ideas from Maria Montessori's *The Child in the Church* as well as from her successor in religious education, Sofia Cavalletti, who wrote *The Religious Potential of the Child*. Both Montessori and Cavalletti worked from within a Roman Catholic perspective. Catherine Stonehouse, in *Joining Children on the Spiritual Journey*, has adapted Berryman's approach to fit more mainstream evangelical churches. Much of what is described here is adapted from Stonehouse's book, and her videotape *Children's Worship*, part of which is available online at http://childfaith.net/stonehouse.html. In addition to Stonehouse's material, I am also indebted to the work of Montessori, Cavalletti, and Berryman for their general framework and perspective.

approach is used. While churches have been the main context for this approach to working with children, it is not hard for parents to adapt.[11]

A key element is to have a space in the house (or perhaps outside your immediate home) that is devoted to the procedure; the child should not be allowed in this area except when the parent and child are participating in Godly Play. The reason for this is that the child is to be quiet and reflective whenever in this "sacred space"; everyday behavior is not tolerated here.

As the child enters this special location, the parent quietly says that this is a special place because this is where she can hear about God, hear from God, and talk with God. This means that she needs to talk and walk slower than normal and be quiet to hear God's voice. The child is told to imagine seeing Jesus come into the room, sitting down next to her. He will listen to whatever she wants to tell him. After a moment of silent prayer, the parent offers a short, audible prayer of thanks. Then the parent tells the child that they will sing a song to Jesus, using hand signs as well as voices. The parent emphasizes that the song will be sung directly to God, much as one prays to God.

After the parent and child have quietly sung the song together, the parent tells a story. Jerome Berryman recommends using special, beautiful wood figurines in telling the story—figurines that are never used outside of the special location.[12] One by one the figurines are taken out of the box in which they are stored, but each is removed with a comment such as "These are very precious and special things." Instead of figurines, Catherine Stonehouse sometimes uses felt figures.

The story used in a first session of Godly Play is the parable of the Good Shepherd.[13] This story begins with the parent's slowly taking out

11. In personal conversation with Jerome Berryman, I mentioned the possibility of adapting the approach for parents, and he told me he saw no reason why it would not work at home as well as it does in church contexts. The description of the procedure that follows is my adaptation of Stonehouse's description in her book *Joining Children on the Spiritual Journey* and her somewhat different procedure illustrated on the videotape.

12. Cathy tells me that the beautifully carved figurines recommended by Jerome Berryman and others who follow this method cost several hundred dollars, but she had some of her graduate students make less costly versions. Perhaps this would be a good project for some of the fathers, mothers, or teenagers at your church, if they have the necessary skill and interest. Jerome speaks of some African tribal children who engage the story using rocks.

13. Jerome found that this story was especially resonant with sick and dying children, as they quickly understood the shepherd to be a source of comfort and care. With

a box that holds the figurines or felt figures, quietly asking, "I wonder what this could be? I wonder if it could be a present. Or it might be a something else. I wonder." Then a sheep is taken out and the parent says, "I wonder what this could be?" The child is likely to say that it is a sheep. Then the parent might ask, "I wonder whose sheep it is? I wonder where the person that owns the sheep is? I wonder why the sheep are here?" and so on. The parent continues taking out the objects and placing them between her and the child, asking "I wonder" questions but encouraging the child to think about the objects rather than to tell who and what they are.

After each of the sheep and finally the Good Shepherd are introduced in his manner, the story is played out by the parent's moving the objects and telling the story. Then a special Bible is brought out and the parent reads the verse that where Jesus says, "I am the Good Shepherd" (John 10:11). The parent quotes the Bible: "My sheep know my voice; I know every one of them by name" (cf. John 10:3, 27), and then gently asks questions such as, "I wonder what the names of these sheep might be? I wonder if they like this place? I wonder how having the Shepherd so close to them makes them feel? I wonder if you have been in dangerous places. I wonder if you knew the Good Shepherd was near you." The figurines or felt drawings are moved and touched by the parent as each of the questions is asked (or as other similar questions are asked). Some time for thinking follows each of these questions.

When the story and Bible reading conclude, each object is individually and carefully put away. The child is told, "Watch, so you can put them away if you decide to work with these today." Again, the actions are done very slowly, to emphasize the special separateness of the location and activity, as well as to provide opportunity for reflection.

At this point the child is given several options for continuing Godly Play, such as taking a few minutes to talk with Jesus quietly, looking at the Bible, drawing a picture that relates to the story, or working with the figurines or objects of the story. While the parent is there to help if called upon, the child is encouraged to work on her own, as God leads. Before the parent and child leave the special area, the parent blesses the child with a comment such as, "It was great to worship here today. Don't forget that the Good Shepherd knows you and even knows your name."

---

more-typical preschoolers, both Jerome and Catherine found that the Good Shepherd parable was also resonant with children.

In subsequent weeks or sessions, the child is allowed to come back to a previous story and play it out with the figurines, or to play out the current story, to draw pictures, or for other possibilities. The child is encouraged to follow his or her own inclinations, as long as play is slow, quiet, and reverent. Some children have a deep encounter with God, but not every child has a profound experience each time Godly Play is used.

The purpose of the approach needs to be kept in mind: this procedure should not be used to impose religion, but rather provide an opportunity for encountering God if God so chooses, and if the child is open to him. (The parent's role is that of an assistant who may need to step out of the way and trust God to connect with the child.) Often children who experience Godly Play" will have a satisfying encounter with God that reaches deeply into the youngsters to produce calm, peace, and joy.

One of the distinctive aspects of this method is a lack of eye contact with the child as the story is told, so that the focus will be on the materials used and on the story itself. Second, there is an atmosphere of reverence, with slow deliberate movements by the parent and later when the child plays out the story alone. Not many responses are solicited from the child; instead she is encouraged to wonder silently and reflect on what happens. The focus of everything is on God and quiet reverence for God.

One of the key questions asked of Catherine Stonehouse about this approach is, how can active little boys handle the slow pace and quiet? Cathy suggests that people often expect boys and sometimes even girls to be rowdy and highly active, but with encouragement and instruction, children can be quiet and reflective. Having a special place that is only used in this manner is one key. Stonehouse comments, "Through stories, children connect with the deep truths about God . . . Lead children into the stories to meet God there."[14] She also includes the lighting of candles for some of the stories, and other quiet activities.

This approach, which almost needs to be seen to be fully appreciated, can be readily adapted to a wide variety of biblical content. What is most crucial is that the child be allowed to play out the story alone, without the parent getting involved in interpreting what is happening. With encouragement toward quiet reflection rather than correct answers to questions, the child becomes more open to God and personal application from the story. On occasion, for example, Jerome and Catherine

14. Stonehouse, *Children's Worship*.

report children saying things such as, "Sometimes I feel like that lost sheep." Or, "The Good Shepherd really keeps me safe"—indications that youngsters are personalizing the story, an ability thought not to develop until the preteen years. Perhaps God bypasses the mental limitations of the child and reveals himself to the child personally when the child is prepared by experiencing the biblical account in playing out the story and is provided a quiet, reflective context.

The Godly Play approach has been used with school-age children as well as preschoolers.[15] This approach may not be for every parent or every child. Indeed, Catherine Stonehouse emphasizes that children need to be ready for the approach, as evidenced by curiosity, strong interest, and questions. It sets the stage for the possibility of a divine encounter with the child.

We suspect it is best to use a variety of approaches with your preschool children, both more active methods as well as more quiet methods like this one. But if Godly Play sparks an interest with you, we encourage you to obtain some of the books and videotapes mentioned in the footnotes for this section and in the bibliography, and then give it a try. Of course, you may also want to develop your own personal variation of this method so that it fits your personality and those of your children. What is most important is that you teach your children about God, somehow give them space to experience God, and then affirm and encourage them in their spiritual walk and experience.

15. Catherine Stonehouse's work has included school-age children as well as preschoolers. Jerome Berryman has authored or helped author several books about Godly Play approach. These include *Teaching Godly Play* (with DVDs and related curricula) and his book with Sonja Stewart: *Young Children and Worship.*

| FOUR |

Salvation

Moment and Memory

Six-year-old Andy was a good boy most of the time, and his mother, Susan, counted herself fortunate that he only argued with her occasionally. He seemed to enjoy his class at church and obviously anticipated his bedtime story each evening. He got along fairly well with the other kids in the neighborhood. But Susan worried a bit about the fact that he had not prayed the sinner's prayer and asked Christ into his heart. She wondered, "Should I talk about this with him, or would that be forcing him to make a decision he is not yet able to make? Does he understand enough to really be a Christian? Even if he does confess his sins and ask forgiveness for them, won't he need a fuller salvation experience when he gets older?"

Susan's questions are important ones that have been considered by theologians and Bible scholars.[1] It could be that a pressured decision made in early childhood could easily be discarded in adolescence as a part of "childish conformity."[2] Yet the eternal consequences of not making a decision for Christ are also potentially horrendous, if Andy is old enough to be responsible for his sin. For centuries theologians have argued about such things as the "age of accountability" when children are held entirely responsible for their own sins. Unfortunately there is

1. For example, see Lawson, "In Right Relationship with God," 108–21; and Issler, "Biblical Perspectives on Developmental Grace," 54–71. Also see the classic sources: Hayes, "Evangelism of Children," 399–415; and Ingle, ed., *Children and Conversion.*

2. The issue of eternal security is probably irrelevant to this matter, since the question of whether the child genuinely accepts Christ as Savior is an internal issue. Those who believe in eternal security would say of the teenager that rejects their earlier affirmation may have made an outward profession without a genuine inner commitment.

no consensus on this topic, and estimates of the "age of accountability" range from age three to the preteen or early teen years!

As noted previously, children may have spiritual experiences prior to salvation, but they do not have the Holy Spirit resident in their lives. As a result, their spiritual experiences are less than what God would ideally like them to have, yet nonetheless are genuine experiences of the spirit realm. God gives light before conversion, and if the child acts upon that light, she or he will move on to the next phase and eventually to salvation.

The Holy Spirit is given at salvation, and thus the Bible speaks of a new life beginning at this point (i.e., life in the Spirit). The Holy Spirit connects the child with God in a new way, as the youngster becomes a child of God, equal to Christian adults in respect to being in relationship with God. The child, like Christian adults, is now a coheir with Christ. God is no longer experienced as outside the child, but now God in the form of the Holy Spirit is within the youngster. Salvation is an experience of God, but it is an experience that transforms permanently.

After salvation, spiritual experiences may come somewhat like the experiences prior to salvation, but now the Holy Spirit is present and guides the believer into all truth and also acts as a Comforter. He is God in us, revealing God's message to youngsters (and to us) in Scripture as well as in a more direct manner through the "still, small voice."

Crisis and Relationship

Both of us grew up attending camp meetings and revival services with our parents. These often emphasized the importance of a crisis experience of salvation, as well as at least one additional crisis after salvation. Many of the times that we went forward during altar calls as children, we sought some crisis—whether to seek salvation again or purification and holiness, or to be a better soul winner or to have more enthusiasm for our faith, or . . . Well, the list is endless, limited only by the imaginations of the evangelists we heard. This might be summarized, "I am bad, God is good; try harder."[3]

We know some of those speakers must have spoken about having a relationship with God, but somehow that relationship did not come

3. Jacobsen, *He Loves Me!* 43.

through as dramatically as the insistence that we needed to come forward. When I (Don) was about five or so, I recall asking my father why evangelists always wanted people to come forward at the end of the services. He must have said something like, "Because there are special blessings for bringing people to Christ." But somehow in my mind I got the idea that God gave the evangelist money for people that came forward. This made a lot of sense to my immature mind, and I grew up to find that it was partly true: not many churches invite (and thus pay for) evangelists who get little response!

Somehow we need to communicate to our children that the initial crisis of asking Christ into your life, while vivid and important, is only the beginning of a journey, which involves a relationship with Christ. However, it could be that the idea of a journey or relationship may be puzzling to children, as they may expect either a literal vacation or regular, interactive conversation with God. One preschooler who was interviewed by a researcher in Europe refused to pray or go to church for five months because she was upset with God. She had said hello to God when she entered the church, but when she heard nothing in reply, she decided that she would not be his friend until he at least greeted her.[4]

Perhaps with small children we need to be careful using these metaphors for living out the Christian life. We might emphasize that God may be a friend, for example, but that he may not be exactly like other friends, because he is not just a human being. This may be an important area where you need to share with your youngster that a relationship with God means that you can talk to him anywhere at any time, but he may or may not respond immediately. We also need to explain that he often speaks to us through the Bible and through the examples of people we know, as well as through the examples of people in the Bible.

The initial crisis can be celebrated regularly, even by having a born-again birthday party—an idea suggested by Cheri Fuller and Christine Yount.[5] While such celebrations can more deeply impress the importance of the decision that has been made, we also must be careful not to make the celebration frivolous and centered on presents. If one of your children has a spiritual birthday and the other does not, there may be subtle pressure to make a decision prematurely. On the other hand, if all

4. Jaspard reports this comment in Tamminen et al., "The Religious Concepts of Preschoolers," 69.

5. Fuller, *Opening Your Child's Spiritual Windows*; and Yount, *With All Their Heart*.

your children have spiritual birthdays, they can all be celebrated, so long as the merriment uplifts Christ rather than the child. It may be equally important to record the date of conversion in the Bible that your child owns. Make the date a "standing stone" (Josh 4:4–7): a memorial that marks a beginning but certainly not the end of one's spiritual walk.

Many theologians are quick to discount the idea of multiple salvation experiences; it seems unlikely that an individual who has been genuinely saved will need to be saved again and again. Many verses of Scripture emphasize the security of the believer. But it can be equally misleading to children and adults to suggest that one vague decision is all there is to salvation. This can produce a false security; indeed, it is possible that a person who looks back to an early "salvation" experience as the only evidence of being a Christian is not saved at all. They could have a false eternal security. If God's grace has brought genuine salvation, the person will be changed, and there will continue to be spiritual growth after the initial conversion experience.

Conversion may be the first time the child meets God, but not the last. The goal is to walk with Christ, not to take a step for God and then walk wherever we wish and hope that God is with us. One of the distinctive elements of Christian spirituality is that conversion results in a new creature with new eyes and the newfound presence of the Holy Spirit, who reveals how God relates to all of life. As the Christian looks at God's special revelation (the Bible), the Holy Spirit teaches us and shows us how Scripture relates to daily situations. Thus the Christian seeks to take faith and relate it to every experience and every relationship. Children can participate in this process as they experience God and as they are nurtured, provided with good examples to follow, and encouraged by parents and teachers.

Balance the idea of a crisis with at least equal emphasis upon the ongoing process of growing spiritually; too many children grow up thinking that a crisis decision is all that is involved in the Christian life. There may be phases and even points of change before salvation and special experiences with God after salvation as well. These come as part of a relationship, and while these experiences may not be as eternally decisive as salvation, they are real and often very meaningful. Children need to understand both the dynamic of everyday life and gradual progress in spiritual growth as well as the special times when one enjoys and appreciates God to an unusual degree—whether such times are frequent or infrequent—in the Christian life.[6]

Salvation at Different Ages

The salvation of a four-year-old will usually be quite different from that of an adult or even of a teenager. When a child grows up in a Christian home and attends church from infancy, she is not as likely to have an earth-shaking crisis (and thus, perhaps, such children especially need to celebrate spiritual birthdays). Indeed some writers have emphasized that children be incorporated into church life from the beginning so that they cannot recall a life without Christ.[7] Tony Campolo speaks of a nine-year-old who gave a testimony of living a life of sin and sorrow until she met the Lord.[8] Obviously, she was just imitating adult testimonies, although certainly she may have been genuinely saved.

Conversions later in life are more likely to be vivid and dramatic changes for the person who turns from a life of sin to a life with Christ. This is not to rule out major changes in one's Christian life even if a child accepts Christ at an early age. For example, the person who decides to move from a Pentecostal church to an Episcopal church may consider the change to be more dramatic than their early conversion![9] Regardless, children need to understand that the Christian life is an ongoing journey likely to be punctuated with moments of significant change and encounters with God.

There is a sense in which salvation is the same for everyone. This gift of God requires admitting sin and receiving forgiveness for that sin. Salvation also produces a change in the person's life, a turning from the old ways and a turning to the ways of the Holy Spirit.

6. See Cheri Fuller's concept of "The Enjoying God Window" in her *Opening Your Child's Spiritual Windows*.

7. This controversial idea was emphasized by Horace Bushnell in *Christian Nurture*. It may be that Bushnell would advocate many minute affirmations over a single crisis event, and indeed this may be the case for Christians who do not recall a singular moment when they were converted. Besides being a well-known preacher and teacher, Bushnell also was the creator of the first public park (see http://www.bushnellpark.org/bushbio.html).

8. Many years ago I heard Tony give this illustration in a message I heard on tape. Unfortunately, I do not know the exact date or location.

9. This is not as absurd as it may sound. A student of mine, a very outspoken Pentecostal when a student, soon after graduation became an Orthodox priest!

But in another sense salvation is different for everyone. We have met people who believed there were three crisis points in the Christian faith: initial grace (salvation), more grace (total dedication), and the highest state of grace (becoming a missionary or pastor). Nonsense! The particular Christian life God has designed for each child and adult is unique; no two Christians are alike or should be alike. The New Testament emphasizes this uniqueness when it describes the spiritual gifts. Not everyone has every gift, because each person fits into the body in a manner consistent with one's personality and abilities.

While each person has a distinctive role in the body of Christ, decisions for Christ may have similarities attributable to the age of the new believers. The young child who receives Christ will experience salvation differently from the adult who is saved. While the degree of change in their lives will probably be different (the adult has a longer history of sin to turn from), the experience of salvation is also likely to be different. This difference comes in part because of the difference in mental maturity. The child does not have the ability to understand all that an adult can understand, and thus this affects the mental understanding of salvation. Now God can, if he so chooses, reveal to children insights into salvation beyond their years, but this is probably uncommon.

The basic requirements for salvation are believing in God, realizing you have sinned and that sin separates you from God, realizing that God has provided a way of forgiveness through the death of Christ on the cross, and finally accepting God's forgiveness and provision for new life through Christ through turning from the old to the new (repentance). Yet the age at which this takes place can make significant differences.

During the prenatal and infancy stages of life, salvation is extremely unlikely. A possible exception was John the Baptist, who was described as filled with the Holy Spirit while still inside his mother (Luke 1:15). Limited ability to reflect on one's life as a whole may limit preschoolers from grasping the concept of giving oneself completely to God, although a number of Christians describe salvation experiences that occurred as early as three or four. If saved during these years, children will probably experience little change from life before salvation to life after, and unless parents help children remember the event, they may not be able to point to a specific day of salvation. The angle of departure from the previous life is small if parents encouraged good, moral living prior to salvation. The eternal direction has changed, and the goal of spiritual maturity will require adjustments throughout life, but such a child will not be drastically different in their behavior on the day before and on the day after salvation. We might say the point of departure is fifteen degrees.

School-age children who become Christians are somewhat different from the youngsters who become Christians earlier. Because they are mentally more mature, they are better able to see the developing patterns of sin in their lives and thus to make a decision to go in another direction. Children at this age do not have ingrained habits of sin, as would an adult, yet the angle of departure from the past is a bit steeper. Thus the change resulting from salvation may be a bit more observable. Some children who are saved at this age, however, may still have a difficult time pinpointing the day of salvation, or exactly what changes are expected of them immediately after salvation. They also have some limitations on their reflective ability, and so they—like those who became Christians as preschoolers—are likely to sense the need for rededication when they become teenagers; they can commit their present lives to Christ during their childhood years, but because of mental limitations they cannot think of the totality of life. As a result, they are unlikely to completely articulate or to fully grasp implications of a life-altering decision to regard Christ's lordship; they are unable to think in global terms, such as committing every moment of their lives and their entire future to Christ. Perhaps here the point of departure on average is forty-five degrees: significant change, but probably not a total reversal.

In adolescence the angle of departure from the past life is more like ninety degrees: a very different direction. One of the characteristics of adolescence is to go contrary to adult expectations. Child-development researchers often point out the tendency of adolescents to think in terms of ideals and of expecting everyone to conform to their ideals.[10] When teens realize that not everyone will do this, and that not everyone will even accept their concept of what is ideal, they may become countercultural in their thinking or appearance, at least for a while.

It is at this stage of life that the ideals of genuine Christianity can be understood, provided that those ideals are presented in a winsome way to the adolescent mind. If the ideals of Christianity are affirmed as an aspect of salvation or of living the Christian life, spiritual growth can be rapid. Yet because of their idealistic acceptance of Christianity, teens may react negatively to parents who are less than ideal, and may possibly

10. Piaget spoke of this tendency in *Six Psychological Studies*.

reject of the institutional church. Christian youth groups and nonchurch Christian groups may be very appealing. There may be some rebellion in the reaction to the church, parents, and society, but teenagers may also be pointing out ideals of the Christian faith that have not been emphasized sufficiently.

In its own way, adolescence is a good age for conversion; the Bible has many ideals that can appeal to adolescence. However, those ideals may require the teenager to turn from the values of peers and the predominant youth culture. If a presentation of the gospel appeals to the ideals of teenagers, it may be effective, but it may be a costly change, and thus youths need the support of key peers and of adults willing to admit they are less than perfect. The new mental abilities of teenagers provide the possibility of a great deal of spiritual insight. But for this potential to be realized requires adults who are open, sympathetic, and perhaps a bit unconventional.

One last concern should be noted related to salvation at different ages. Sometimes guest preachers at churches and at other religious meetings speak of the major changes they made upon becoming a Christian. This can make children and youths a bit envious, especially those who became Christians early in life. The testimony of kids raised in the church will not be as dramatic, and thus these may feel they do not have much of a testimony. As adults we can realize that they have many advantages by having years of faithful living, even though it makes for a less exciting testimony. Perhaps it is not too much to suggest that those who have the dramatic testimonies should (and often do) also express regret that they did not become Christians earlier in life. We can also encourage these children not to become wayward during their teen years; even though they can return as did the prodigal, they will have missed out on much; and by having strayed from their earlier faith, they may have additional problems that can be with them the rest of their lives.

Stages before Salvation

Salvation rarely takes place without the child (or adult) going through some preparatory stages.[11] Initially there must be an awareness that a

11. These stages are adapted from Engel and Norton, *What's Gone Wrong with the Harvest?* These are considered in relation to spiritual growth in general in my article "Stages of Spiritual Development: Crisis Experiences in the Christian Life."

supreme being exists, then an initial awareness of the gospel message. Once the child has grasped the implications of the gospel message, the child must develop a receptive, positive attitude towards that message of hope. Next the child must recognize the sin in his or her own life. Then a decision must be made to act upon that recognition, and finally the individual repents by changing the course of life through trusting Christ. Jesus used the metaphor of plant growth to describe spiritual development, including planting seeds, cultivating growth, and so on. Similarly, the "seeds" planted in children need to be encouraged, as the child progresses through the stages.

Awareness of sin and consciousness of guilt is a crucial necessity for children before they can accept Christ. Some psychologists and educators today emphasize the need to be rid of guilt, but in reality some personal guilt is necessary for salvation. How can we instill desirable guilt for genuine wrongdoing without our children's developing excessive guilt, in which they feel guilty for things that are not sinful? What can you do to help your child have a conscience that is not overly sensitive but is also sufficient to produce an awareness of personal sin and thus of a need for salvation?

The research gives us fairly clear answers to these questions.[12] It is important that children of all ages, but especially preschoolers, have expectations and limits imposed by parents and other adults. The limits or rules should be as consistent as possible across situations and also consistently enforced, especially by parents. When parents combine a general atmosphere of love and affection for children with reasonable discipline for disobedience, their youngsters are more likely to develop a conscience and feel guilt when they violate the rules. Guilt comes from the fear of losing parental love, and thus the child tends to internalize their standards to avoid dealing with guilt. Again, the key age is the preschool years, from two to about six years of age, for developing a conscience that produces guilt when the child has genuinely done wrong.

12. The conclusions in these paragraphs are primarily from dozens of research studies related to moral-development research and research of parenting styles and conscience development. See Wallinga and Skeen, "Physical, Language, and Social-Emotional Development," 38–39; see Massey, "Preschooler Moral Development," 90. See also Buzzelli and Walsh, "Discipline, Development, and Spiritual Growth," 158–59; Aldridge and Box, "Moral and Affective Dimensions of Childhood," 88; Ratcliff, "Parenting and Religious Education," 67; and Meier and Ratcliff, *Raising Your Child*, 34–35, 110, 124–25, 144–45.

Too many rules can result in the parent's needing to discipline much of the time, and it is possible that the parent will just give up and not discipline even for things that are clearly wrong. It can also help to talk with the child about the feelings of others, including the parents' feelings, to help the child develop empathy (feeling something of what others feel). Some children seem to be more sensitive than others to parental reproof and discussion of how other people feel. I recall one of our children talked back to me at about age four, and I (Don) sat down with my child and explained that what was said hurt me inside. The youngster burst into tears, asking for forgiveness and saying how sorry s/he was. I knew that child well enough to know this was unusual behavior and that the expression was genuine. I know there are other kinds of children who would not be so sensitive, and they would probably respond better to discipline for misdeeds.

Development of guilt for misdeeds is also likely when a number of different methods of reasonable forms of discipline are used, as well as reproof and talking about the feelings of others, although some evidence suggests that such discussions are more likely to be effective with older children than with preschoolers. Moral-development theory says that children tend to be focused upon punishment for doing wrong during the preschool years, then during the school-age years they tend to focus on the positive rewards for doing good as well as punishment for wrongdoing. By age nine or ten, youngsters begin thinking more and more about the social approval of both adults and peers, but occasionally continue to reflect upon punishment and rewards for their actions. Children of all ages are also powerfully influenced by observing others who express guilt over doing wrong.

While guilt and sin have sometimes been put down by some psychologists and educators, usually because these are emphasized too much by some rigid and oppressive parents, good research does show that children who have religious beliefs and awareness of personal sin are more likely to have healthy self-development.[13] Guilt, an understanding of sin, and the experience of forgiveness grow out of a child's experiences of parental love and authority, and especially parents' reactions to the child's successes and failures. In contrast poor parents fall short in expressing love to their children, do not take an adequate level of authority, or threaten the child with punishment from God for bad behavior.

13. The conclusions in this paragraph are from Kenneth Hyde's *Religion in Childhood and Adolescence*, 204, 218, 231–32.

Some Suggested Guidelines on Leading a Child to Christ

Edward Hayes recommends that we encourage our child to have faith is Jesus by building a foundation for salvation and discipleship based upon love from the first day of life outside the womb.[14] As Paul wrote, "From infancy you have known the holy Scriptures, which are able to make you wise for salvation through faith in Christ Jesus" (2 Tim 3:15).

Hayes suggests that we not make children anxious in the appeal for salvation. The Holy Spirit should do the convicting and motivating toward salvation, and excessive human efforts can interfere with God's timetable. We should let the Holy Spirit lead children to a decision rather than forcing it upon youngsters. Similarly, Cheri Fuller comments that we are not in control of salvation; thus we are called to embrace the child's spiritual journey and realize that the youngster may open the heart to Christ at the least expected time.[15]

Parents can teach that every action is accountable to God, not just to people. However, the Bible is clear that younger children are primarily accountable to parents (Eph 6:1–2). Hayes also comments that any appeal for the child to accept Christ as Savior be made privately, in a simple manner, and from pure motives (in other words, not because the parent wants to brag about leading the child to Christ). Of course, we allow the child to ask questions, and Christine Yount adds that the parent ask questions to clarify whether the child understands salvation, especially open-ended questions, that cannot be answered with just a yes or no but that rather questions that stimulate dialogue.[16]

While he does not provide a formula for parents in leading a child to Christ, Hayes suggests that the youngster be asked to accept Christ internally ("Tell yourself, 'Jesus, I ask that you will become my Savior'") before requesting that the child give an outward affirmation. He also suggests we wait for the child to initiate by asking, "How do I become a Christian?" and that we not make what is required too easy; acknowledgment of the decision before others helps the child keep the experience clearly in mind.

What is involved in asking a child to accept Christ? Hayes states that the child needs to understand why Jesus died on the cross.

---

14. See Hayes, "Evangelism of Children."
15. Fuller, *Opening Your Child's Spiritual Windows*, 122.
16. Yount, *With All Their Heart*, 29

Specifically, that his death shows his love for us, that he paid for the sins that we commit, and that we must confess that we sin and ask for forgiveness. Reading Scriptures such as John 3:16; John 3:36; Romans 3:23; and Romans 5:6 is recommended, and explaining the unknown or difficult terminology for the child. The analogies of becoming part of a family (John 1:12), of being born a second time (John 3:3), of receiving a gift, or of being freed from prison are more useful than the commonly used phrase, "receiving Jesus into your heart." Christine Yount likewise recommends using ideas that are very concrete, such as being adopted into God's family and becoming God's child.

Christine Yount recommends some less commonly used Scriptures with children, including Hezekiah's comment that we must dedicate ourselves to God (2 Chr 29:31).[17] Another scriptural passage suggests that the heart, rather than outward behavior, is central to repentance (Joel 2:13). However, confession of faith before others as well as inner belief are essential for salvation (Rom 10:9–10).

Because the understanding of salvation may be limited in early childhood, Cheri Fuller suggests that salvation may come in two or more phases that involve the child's growing awareness of the need for forgiveness, the child's asking Christ to control and guide future plans, and the child's surrendering to Christ additional areas of life.[18]

Cheri Fuller also recommends that we not elevate biblical characters as ideals (with the exception of Jesus, of course), nor should we talk as if certain adults are perfect. However, we should encourage adults to share with children the stories of their faith in God, including adults who have strayed from a close relationship with God and then returned. Note for the child that many people experience the unpleasant and even devastating consequences of waywardness. Yet the goal is for the child to own her or his faith, not have a faith borrowed from parents, pastor, or friends.

17. Yount, *With All Their Heart*, 22
18. Fuller, *Opening Your Child's Spiritual Windows*, 125

| FIVE | # Cocreating Life in God
You, Your School-Age Children,
and God

*It was the first day of school for our first child.
The bright yellow bus stopped to pick up our son,
and he was excited to discover what lay ahead
for him. We were a bit less excited. It struck us
that we had done our best for six years to instill a
strong faith tradition and would continue to do
so in the years ahead. Yet we also knew that with
the school bus came the influence of new friends
and teachers who might also impact that faith.
We prayed that God would protect him, and provide Christian friends that would help him.*

A CENTRAL THEME TO THIS book is that you and your child can
benefit each other as you grow in Christ. The two of you together
are more than the two of you apart. God designed us to share with one
another, and children are not second-rate Christians who are excluded
from helping others grow spiritually. Indeed, as we have seen before,
God intends us to learn from children, and we believe this includes our
own children.[1]

In my (Don's) graduate education I learned quite a bit about child
development. All three of my graduate degrees included courses about
children, with emphasis upon preschoolers with my first degree and
more on school-aged children with the other two. My doctoral research
involved studying youngsters from kindergarten through sixth grade,

1. Boyatzis, in "The Co-construction of Spiritual Meaning in Parent-Child Communication," 180–200; his chapter of a book I edited (*Children's Spirituality*), researched
this idea of parents and children coconstructing spiritual meaning. I recall thinking
about this idea at approximately the same time he was doing his research and sharing
this mutual interest at a conference. I do not recall which of us thought of the idea first,
but I am grateful for the fine work he did on the topic.

and I interviewed more than fifty children who were in the third, fourth, and fifth grades. In addition, I taught child development at the college level for many years and even wrote and helped write a number of books on children. And yet my children continue to surprise me. I am sure I learned more about kids from my own children than I did from any book I read. They are complex creatures who can humble a scholar very quickly.

What Is It Like to Be a Child?

We adults often think of children as a "them" that are rather unlike us. This is accentuated by some child psychologists who talk almost as if children are a completely different species from adults. They are different in some ways, but we have much in common as well.

We have all been children. We experienced life as a child. Yet most of us have lost our child perspective. As adults, we reflect upon children from a different perspective, using adult thought, not the thinking of children. Even most researchers and educators look at children and childhood from adult perspectives. Can you imagine a child who could describe herself as Piaget, Skinner, or (Lord, help us) Freud viewed youngsters? Of course not! While those theories may be accurate at least in some respects they certainly do not reflect how children look at the world; they reflect how educated adults think about children. Parents do this as well; we usually take a parental perspective rather than attempting to understand the child's view of the world.

We cannot completely shed an adult perspective, and perhaps there is some advantage to this; some adult views of children are useful and helpful. There are valuable things to learn from theorists and researchers. But life for a child is not always the way adults think children experience it. We need to comprehend the lived experience of childhood, as it is embedded in their everyday lives. Adults need to embark upon a quest for an insider's view of childhood, rather than the adult, outsider's view.

One interesting and valuable attempt to accomplish this goal is to examine youngsters from the vantage point of child culture (sometimes termed peer culture). This view emphasizes that children build their own subculture, which is often in opposition—or at least quite different from—the predominant culture of the school, home, and church. An important component of child culture includes "child folklore," which includes riddles and knock-knock jokes, as well as poems and songs used during games such as jump rope. Graffiti often reflects child culture. The rough-and-tumble play of boys (and some girls), in which they punch and wrestle playfully, is also a staple of child culture. Child culture also includes private ridicule of teachers and school and the secrets shared by friends. Child culture is often critical of children of the opposite sex, reflected in the accusation that they have cooties, smell bad, or have other repugnant characteristics. It is a culture reflected in belching competitions, flatulence contests, and daring bicycle tricks.

Why is child culture important? There is only one reason: because it is important to children. It is one of those aspects of being a child that most of us have forgotten (or try to forget!). But as adults we quickly recognize it, although our faces may redden a bit in the process. Child culture is something most children experience every day of their lives.

But don't be misled; child culture is not the destination of our quest to remember childhood. We have probably forgotten, or at least have suppressed from memory, other aspects of childhood as well. Think of the times you were painfully embarrassed because you forgot an important assignment. Recall the times the kids laughed at you for some misspoken word or thoughtless mistake. Remember the time you first rode in a convertible, or made mud pies, tasted that first banana, or took your first communion. Don't forget the combination of agony and anticipation related to your first love, the love you didn't dare confess to your friends, or confessed to your best friend as one of your deepest secrets.

The road back to childhood is familiar; we just haven't traveled it for a few years. The actual experience of childhood is perhaps forgotten, or more likely our memories have been modified by adult experience. As Scripture says, it is valuable to once again "become as little children" (Matt 18:2, KJV).

What is it like to be a child? No adult can think exactly like a child. But perhaps we can recapture a bit of that experience by listening to children, letting them speak freely of their thoughts and actions, without criticizing or condemning. We need to let ourselves try to remember, and attempt to recall the experience of being a child without the constraints of adult logic and insight. It is difficult, but if we can at least partially succeed, we will better understand our youngsters. We may be able to approximate the experience of "seeing with the eyes of a child."

Sharing Yourself with Your Children

As we attempt to remember what it is like to be in the shoes of our children, we also need to share ourselves with kids. While children are different from us, we also have much in common. As we apply truths from the Bible to our own lives, we may see parallels for children. And many of us will quickly admit that when we try to relate the Bible to our children's lives, the Lord often taps us on the shoulder and reminds us that we need that idea too.

We realize you cannot tell your children all of your problems. Indeed, parents who share all their woes and difficulties give their children burdens that they are not equipped to share. However, you can at least occasionally share areas where God is teaching you and shaping you, and the fact that you are still learning may be a surprise to your child. Often children, especially younger children, look to adults as perfect or nearly perfect, and we parents often don't want to shake their impression. It's kind of nice to be thought of as nearly God. The problem is, it isn't true. We aren't that great; we all have a good bit to learn. So, while it is humbling, it may be a good thing to share some of our struggles with the children.

Of course the age of the children will have an impact upon what we tell our youngsters. With preschoolers we might briefly share something that is a bit similar to what they are experiencing, or we can talk about things we struggled with when we were young. If you plan to talk about the past, you had better talk soon, because it won't be long before those listening ears will be older and won't want to hear those stories.

There is a place to share your own spiritual growth with your children. And it isn't fair to only tell about the events where you have had victory. Ongoing struggles that are not too much for your children should be shared, even if it is humbling. Ask them to pray for you, and don't be too surprised when they do so out loud, perhaps right then. Again, don't give them heavy burdens, but share something real and true about your own struggles.

Draw out the parallels between your life and your child's. When your children tell you of the bullies at school, listen and hear them at the deepest level. If appropriate, do what you can to help them, including contacting the teacher or principal if need be. After you have heard them and have conveyed to them that you heard, you might ask for prayer about the bullies in your life. Listen carefully as they tell you about a struggle with the teacher, and try to put yourself in their shoes. Then after they know that you have heard them, you can also share some of your own struggles with a friend. Difficulties with their friends may have parallels to some of the problems you are having with your friends. Homework for the kids has its parallel in work brought home from the office.

Now there are things you can tell a school-aged child who is able to keep confidences that you might not tell your preschooler. Perhaps the preschooler needs fewer details. And there are some issues that are strictly taboo to share with your children, such as disagreements with the spouse and very private matters. But to show that you value their prayers speaks loudly about your dependence upon God and the common ground you share as fellow believers. Even if you cannot tell your child all the details, you can share more generally or at least can say you have an unspoken prayer request. Your children need to know that there are continuities across the lifespan in relation to many issues and relationships, so they can feel less alone in their struggles and see that what they learn now may influence their future lives as adults.

We recall one of our children telling us of being put down by older children at church.[2] We suggested that he tell them that their comments hurt and to ask if Jesus would do that. Then just leave them alone. We know kids sometimes just have to cope with teasing. But we believe there is also a time for the parent to intervene and to speak either to the other children or to their parents. Parents also need to find parallels between our lives and our children's lives, as well as between the lives of biblical characters and our own lives, and share them with our children.

At times, perhaps, you can share with an older child even the "valley" experiences in life. This is captured in Scripture in the desperation of Job in the ninth chapter of that book. He felt desperation, aloneness, a sense that God had abandoned him. Sharing some of the struggle during the "dark night of the soul" may prompt words of encouragement from the child, reminding us of God's love (although a youngster may be naïve in thinking such reminders will immediately lift you out of the valley). Children need to see a bit of those difficult times we have, because they too go through such valleys. Sometimes adults feel they should shield the child from the reality of dark times when God seems to be out of the picture. Then we wonder why children lose out when they have such

2. See Ronald Cram's excellent *Bullying: A Spiritual Crisis*.

times; they do not expect them, because they may not have seen them in our experience, and thus they do not know how to cope. Shielding them by "putting on a happy face" is less than honest; it is an integrity issue.

While we should not share all of our feelings to the extreme, we should let our children in on the experience to a limited extent. We can speak of "tribulation producing patience" (cf. Rom 5:3) even though we may struggle with believing those words; our times of being discouraged can be a time of teaching not only for ourselves but also for our children. We may even want to talk about Jesus in the wilderness, being tempted by Satan to give in to the Enemy's plans, yet emphasize that a stronger faith results when we resist temptation. Most older children understand the reality of temptation, and their prayers may be a source of strength for us. Even if you try to keep it from your kids, the kids probably know something is wrong; giving them a few details may actually reduce their anxiety about what is happening.

Some children go through extraordinarily hard places, and the openness with which you share your struggles may encourage your child to share his upheavals. We think, for example, of our own son who was found to have an eye abnormality that required several surgeries as well as lengthy CAT scans and MRI scans. He was able to share with us some of his doubts about faith, and the struggles to understand why he had to go through with this. But he also saw how we and the surgeon were able to talk briefly about faith, leaving a deep impression on this woman of Jewish faith, because we shared how we celebrated the Jewish holidays. Similarly, a friend's child had numerous heart surgeries, beginning early in his life. Yet he also realizes God used his witness of faith to doctors and nurses on dozens of occasions as opportunities for hearing about Christ that the medical people may not have had otherwise. Jerome Berryman describes crises of faith of dying and seriously ill children when he was a hospital chaplain, and what great comfort and strength they found in hearing the parable of the Good Shepherd. He also speaks of how those children encouraged family members and other dying children by sharing the unusually deep insights they had from the parable.[3] While we must not minimize the struggles and difficulties of children, we can also

3. A few of these are described in Jerome's *Godly Play*, but more detail is provided in "The Rite of Anointing and Pastoral Care of Sick Children"; also in "The Chaplain's Strange Language: A Unique Contribution to the Health Care Team," 15–40; and in "Religious Images, Sick Children and Health Care" 19–31.

see how God uses such tragic situations, and how children grow spiritually as a result.

Spiritual Spirals

As we look at our child in relationship to a principle he or she is learning or an experience that he or she is undergoing, in a sense we participate at a very different stage of life. As adults rather than children, we are better able (we hope) to understand both the Bible and the events of our lives (because of our ability to think abstractly) as well as the many other experiences we have had, which children have not. Yet time and again we find that our lives are like a spiral, retouching some of the same ideas and experiences, each time adding a new level of understanding and sensitivity.

For example, a number of times during my life I (Don) have been impressed with the biblical concept of the fear of God. When I was a child, I thought of that fear as quite literal: I "shook in my boots" during invitations to come forward for salvation at church. Perhaps I was afraid of going to hell if I didn't go forward one more time, or that everyone else would be raptured and I would be left behind. I also heard my parents talk about someone's having the "fear of God" put in them because one's personal problems were discovered.

As a teenager, I didn't care for this idea of the fear of God, but I knew it meant that I needed to be careful of what I did. I got involved with the wrong crowd during high school and did some things that were illegal, but the fear of God kept me from going very far in the wrong direction. I'm sure praying parents and working at a Christian radio station also helped me from being a full-blown prodigal. Perhaps my having heard the story of the prodigal son also curbed my degree of waywardness.

In college I again came in to contact with the idea of the fear of God when I had Bible teachers who told me *fear* meant "reverence." While God is a friend, we relate to him with limited casualness. There must be a reverent respect for God.

Since then, I have thought of the fear of God several more times. I now think of the fear of God as being the awe of God, not dreading him or expecting pain from him. He is very "Other," more complex than any theology can completely represent. The prospect of friendship with such an "Other" is overwhelming at times; indeed it is beyond my comprehension to think that God cares about me and is personally involved in my life, as well as with millions of other people on our planet. Yet, I also believe reverence is important, as I learned in college, because God is not "my best buddy;" He is the Creator of the universe, and Lord of my life. And I also think the fear of God should keep us from behavior at the edges of what is right, and perhaps I can agree that some people should literally fear what God will do at the final judgment. All these represent different cycles in the spiral to understand the idea of the fear of God. Each spiral adds levels of understanding with every turn.

The spiral can connect with my child as I can revisit my earlier understandings through the eyes of my child. My goal is not to bring the child to my current level of understanding; that will require several more spirals in his or her life. But I can understand where my youngster is, because I was there only a few years ago. (Well, okay, more than a few years!)

Now not everything I learn is on the spiral; I may have a first-time experience with my child, who is also having a first-time experience. This occurred when my young family first went to the beach, an experience that I do not recall ever having in my own childhood. On the other hand, I understand some spirals for the first time when my child experiences them the first time; I didn't get something the first time around, but now I understand, and so does my child. For example, I hated exercise in high school and afterward, and thus disliked the athletic metaphors Paul uses in the New Testament. In the last few years, however, I discovered that my life would probably be shorter and less healthy if I didn't exercise. So I exercise, and Paul's metaphors mean more to me. While this was a repeated spiral (I heard such warnings earlier but didn't take them seriously), this time I really got it. When my children were young they sometimes accompanied me when I exercised: my daughter rollerblading alongside me as I ran, or one of my sons slowing their pace of running to stay next to me. I thank God that they can appreciate those athletic metaphors of Paul the first time around. They can learn from my understanding of a metaphor, and I can learn from their insights about it as well. It is a reciprocal, give-and-take learning experience.

Then at times they spiral, and I learn for the first time. This is harder for my kids because they have been here before, have learned what was intended, and now they are back again at an advanced level while I am learning something for the first time. It is sometimes a struggle as parents to realize that your child may have advanced insight (even a spiritual insight) that you are just now learning. The best example we can think of is when we are filled with turmoil because something breaks down, such as the bathroom commode's overflowing.

"Now what do we do?" is sometimes as much a plea to God as to anyone else. Then we are humbled when one of the kids says, "Well, why not pray?"

Perhaps a moment or two in prayer, as we gather our thoughts, is more beneficial than scurrying around trying to find a telephone book to call Roto-Rooter. Indeed, with a moment or two of reflection and prayer, we might realize using a plunger comes before calling the repairman!

Similarly I (Brenda) was dreading a trip to the dentist, and shared this fear with one of our children. He immediately placed his hand on me and began to pray that God would remove the fear. Indeed his prayers did relieve some of the fear, and with tears in my eyes I hugged my son. Not only did he help relieve my fear, but he also saw himself as having a part in my spiritual advancement. He was not just my child; he was also a brother in Christ.

Indeed, when we learn from our children and their previous spirals, we may be coming close to what Jesus meant when he said those famous words: words that may have a fresh meaning with this new spiral of hearing them: "The disciples came to Jesus and asked, 'Who is the greatest in the kingdom of heaven?' He called a little child and had him stand among them. And he said: 'I tell you the truth, unless you change and become like little children, you will never enter the kingdom of heaven. Therefore, whoever humbles himself like this child is the greatest in the kingdom of heaven. And whoever welcomes a little child like this in my name welcomes me'" (Matt 18:1–5).

The passage goes on with warnings about causing children to sin. But the key principles Jesus was teaching are the need to change, the examples children give us, the requirement of humility, and the blessing of welcoming our children as we would Christ. Sometimes God can teach us through our children if we have adequate humility and a willingness to change as needed.

Reciprocal Discipleship

Young children often have a special sensitivity to God. As we saw in an earlier chapter, this sensitivity may become hardened because of teasing by friends, teachers, or even church people who chuckle or even laugh when the youngster claims God told her something, or that she saw an angel. We need to counter that pressure by listening and not automatically discounting such reports. We may not believe everything they say, as children do have active imaginations. But we should not automatically reject such reports just because they fall outside our current realm of experience. The Bible says to "test the spirits to see if they are from God," not immediately discount or reject the report (1 John 4:1).

Encouraging sensitivity to the Spirit of God is something we can do for our children, and they can do for us. We need to open ourselves to them and to the Holy Spirit, affirming what is biblical and consistent with our faith. Sometimes we forget how much of the supernatural is in the Bible, as we get caught up in day-to-day living. We must not be practicing atheists, living much like those who have no faith in God, as if there were no genuine angels and miracles in life. Too many Christians live their lives as if there were no resurrection; they live the earthly realm with little awareness of or concern about the spiritual realm.

We can also use the spiritual disciplines with our children. For example, the Bible speaks of confessing our sins one to another, which is one of the spiritual disciplines.[4] We are not suggesting that we tell all our sins to our children. But with proper caution, we might confess a few sins that they will understand. When reading the newspaper I (Don) find myself desiring some of the electronic toys I see advertised. These are things I do not need, and at the current prices they are out of the question for our family budget. I know my repeated viewing of the ads is encouraging that desire. I want what the store has; I envy.

Now I realize our children also envy. They too want what they cannot afford, and they often let me know about it. Perhaps they will be more likely to share some of their sins if I confess to them my sin of envy. I can also ask for their prayers that I will not spend so much time looking at and desiring something I should not have, and that I be content with what I have. Those are all things our children could do as well, but it may be that God will speak to their hearts about their sins if I will share with them how God has spoken to me about my sins.

4. Klaus Issler describes many of the spiritual disciplines in his excellent book on living the Christian life, titled *Wasting Time with God*. This is one of the most stirring books I have ever read, affirming many things we take for granted in the Christian life while underscoring some aspects that I had not considered seriously in the past. How I wish I had been able to read this book as a teenager or young adult!

The same can be said about some of the other spiritual disciplines: special times of prayer, meditation, journaling, solitude, and even fasting. Perhaps these will not be as extensive for children: instead of a total fast, you might suggest that your child fast from sweets for a day. Similarly, practicing solitude might be for an hour instead of a day or two for a school-age child. What is most important is that the children want to follow your example in practicing the spiritual disciplines. Ideally your children request participation. The disciplines should never be mandatory. This may be an area that is new to you (and please read up on the practices before attempting them), and it most likely will be a new experience for your child as well. Sharing some of the things you learn in the process can be a source of mutual encouragement to both of you. Listen to your child's insights as well.

Another area of reciprocal discipleship is a time of honest evaluation. This may not be appropriate for every child, and some parents may question the value of this procedure as a whole. If it is attempted, we believe this should be prefaced by prayer and personal reflection—both individually and with your spouse. Probably this should be done one to one with your child, and preferably during two different sessions.

Prior to the first session, tell your child that you want to meet to talk about your job as a parent. When you meet together, pray and ask for God's guidance for your child as well as for an openness on your part. Then ask your child to talk about what he or she likes and doesn't like about your role as a parent. This makes you vulnerable as a parent but also admits that we make mistakes and can overlook problems obvious to others. You might even mention that we are all accountable to God, and thus it is important for you to know how you are doing as a parent.

Consider whether there is any exasperation reflected in your child's comments. The Bible is very clear that we should avoid anything that produces exasperation in our children (Eph 6:4). We should also look for any indication of bitterness, as we may be the cause of this as well (Col 3:21). We should look for indications of these kinds of mistakes throughout our parenting experience, but it may be worthwhile to have such a special time together to do such an assessment.

The reciprocal part of this procedure is to have a second meeting in which the parent describes the strengths and weaknesses of the child. Some parents may not need this second session, as the child may have heard more than enough about these in the day-to-day existence of parent and child. However, the session may still be valuable so that at least equal time can be spent describing the positive attributes of the child in contrast with their weaknesses. If you do talk about the child's areas of need, speak of them as "places to grow" and suggest steps reasonable for the child's level of maturity and ability.

I (Don) tried this procedure a time or two when my children were younger. They seemed a bit surprised that I would ask for such feedback. My one son spoke about the things he appreciated about me, and then mentioned a couple of events that bothered him. I was pleased to hear him bring up the specifics, and we talked them through to our mutual understanding. I do not recall if I apologized, but I suspect I did if it was needed; I have tried to apologize when I blow it as a parent, and I think my kids have more respect for me because of this. My other son was even more positive about me during an evaluation session," and as I recall he had very little criticism to share. However, he has always been one that comes to me with any problem between us, so I was not surprised with the more positive report. This difference arose, I believe, because the personalities of my sons are quite different. I also talked with my daughter, but I do not recall anything of her response. She was quite young at the time, so she may have just told me she loved me, or perhaps she told me she wanted more stuffed animals! Because I tried this procedure a couple times, I found that my children were subsequently more open to share problems and tensions with me in the day-to-day environment. I think they realized I honestly wanted to hear their opinions. But I must confess I am overdue for another evaluation from them!

It is imperative that parents be authentic in this and in the other areas involved in cocreating spiritual life with your child. One cannot talk one way and act another, and then expect the children to be honest and forthright. The way one acts in front of Christians and before the church should match life in the household and job. A lack of Christian authenticity in a previous generation may explain why the second and third generations successively move away from the faith of first-generation Christians.[5] Too often the children of vibrant Christians go to church but fail to live the Christian life outside the church doors. This is often

---

5. Bruce Wilkinson speaks of this generation effect by using three chairs—see his chapter called "Leaving a Legacy," 131–46. Also see Bruce Wilkinson's book *Experiencing Spiritual Breakthroughs*.

due to the lack of a personal walk with God. Thus the third generation sees their faith as an empty shell and rejects it completely.

Unfortunately, many pastors and other church leaders easily fall into such a superficial level of living as they try to please people in the organization instead of keeping biblical principles at the forefront of every relationship and every activity. It is quite easy for their children to reject the façade of the second-generation Christians. The solution, of course, is for every generation to be a first generation, without compromise, and with a comparative lack of duplicity. That takes an openness to God and others that results in a genuine, consistent walk with the Lord. Compromises of our integrity can come at the cost of our children's souls.

Putting a Child's Faith (and Yours) into Action

James 1:27 reminds us that genuine spirituality involves reaching out to others who need our help. One landmark study of what most influences a youngster's faith development found that three elements were crucial: discussing faith with one or both parents, having a regular time of devotions either with the family or a parent, and being involved in a service project with the family.[6] A relationship with God should naturally move us to love and care for those who need our help.

Children need to be with us as we reach out to the unfortunate. Not only can you bring your youngsters with you, but it is a good idea to have them participate actively in some way to help the homeless, the poor, the abused or neglected, the elderly, the infirm, or those who are wayward or lost. For example, as you visit a nursing home (a location that always needs people to help lead church services and minister individually to the elderly), your child can give a testimony. They can also go with you to talk with people in their rooms, listening and loving those who often have been neglected by their own families. My mother moved to a nursing home shortly before she died. Our children benefited from visiting her, but we also saw volunteers bring their children, and often those children were a real joy to the elderly.

You may also volunteer in your church or in another organization for activities that include your children. For example, churches sometimes run soup kitchens for the needy, distribute bread to the poor, or have

6. Roehlkepartain, *The Teaching Church*, 170.

other service projects. Many churches offer older children and teenagers trips to third-world countries, which can powerfully affect older children, even for a lifetime, as they see how people in these countries live. You may speak at length about how other children have little or nothing, but until your child actually sees it first hand, it may just be words to them. We recall Tony Campolo's talking about how his children decided to give up having big gifts at Christmas so they could send the money to an orphanage in Haiti. Years later, when they visited the orphanage, his children were moved to tears because of the joy from helping the helpless.[7]

It may also be good for your children to watch—with you—some videos of adults and children who are starving, abused, or persecuted. These are readily available at minimal cost.[8] These videos may move them—and us—to tears, and hopefully will move us to sacrifice money as well. Children need to see us write checks to support missionaries that are winning the lost and caring for desperate people overseas, in the inner cities, in poor rural areas, and on Native American reservations. Kids need to see us take a turn at teaching the Sunday-school class for preschoolers (older children might assist us in the task) or see us sing in an outreach group. They need to hear us talk about our concern for the lost who face eternity without God, and see us act upon that concern in concrete ways that will help people physically, emotionally, and spiritually. They can write to and pray for the Compassion or World Vision child or children that we support. The specific avenue of service is less important than the fact that we do the task with our children.

As you share your experiences and your faith walk with your child, you are both likely to grow more spiritually than either of you would alone. As Prov 27:17 says, "As iron sharpens iron, so one person is sharpened by another." We are to not forsake the assembling together (Heb 10:25) as Christians, because we can help one another. It is in the close relationships of the family that this can be the case to an even greater extent than in church, if we are open to allowing God to do the creating (and to cocreating with our children) the good work in us that he desires to complete (Phil 1:6).

7. Compolo and Ratcliff, "Activist Youth Ministry," 257–74.

8. Organizations such as Phillis Kilbourn's Rainbows of Hope (a division of WEC International) and other similar organizations have books, videotapes, and regular newsletters and magazines about such issues (online: http://www.rainbowsofhope.org).

| SIX | # Telling, Enacting, and Applying Bible Stories

PARENTS OFTEN STRUGGLE TO have some kind of "family devotions." Many of us never had this experience when we were children. Others of us had very negative experiences as youngsters, listening to long accounts of events that had no relevance to us, and trying to endure lengthy prayers that were equally boring. Today there is great competition for the time of both children and adults, and media that can actively compete for the child's imagination. How can we captivate the spiritual imagination while avoiding boredom and disappointment—for both children and parents?

Bible stories are a staple of ministry to children in church, and in addition to mealtime and bedtime prayers, they tend to be the staple of many Christian homes as well. I (Don) vividly recall the closeness and warmth of my father's reading Bible storybooks, beginning early in my life. He continued to read to me each night until I became "too old for that" (probably in my preteen years). Hearing those stories underscored the importance of the Bible to my parents; I realized at some level that this was a special time, and that the Bible was a special book. Some of my strongest emotions are associated with those times of love expressed by the amount of time given to stories. They probably made it easier for me to talk to them about theology, church, and living for Christ in my teen years and afterward. The evening Bible story was a special time of bonding between us. I also liked the implicit reward of getting to stay up past my regular bedtime as my dad told the stories.

Effective Storytelling

Stories can be read in a deadening manner, and children will very quickly tire of them. Why listen to boring stories when there are videos and

Christian TV programs for children? If the choice is between boredom and high-interest in biblical accounts, it's hard to make a case for the story. But we can learn to tell stories effectively, and stories told and read can be better than the screen versions. How can that be? The reason is that a child must imagine the scene, create a mental picture of what is happening when being told a story. Thus they are not passively receiving the image and sound, as with television and movies. When told well, a story draws the listener into the drama and the mind paints pictures of what is described (a few pictures in the book may help younger children in their "painting").

You can learn to use expression in your voice, which conveys your own interest in the story as well as the desire to make it interesting for children. Practice reading a paragraph when you are alone. First try to vary the pitch in extreme ways, so your voice gets very high and then very low. While the extremes may sound funny, good storytellers make dramatic variations in pitch as they read, usually—though not always—ending the sentence with a lower pitch. Use your high and low variations to bring emphasis to the important words in a sentence. You can also vary the pitch when dialogue occurs, using a higher pitch for female characters and a lower pitch for male characters. You can overdo this and the story will become silly, but some variation helps keep interest and improves comprehension.

The timbre of the voice is also important, with strength or weakness conveyed through the softness or harshness of the voice. Again this should vary by character, with rougher characters given harsher voices, and kinder characters given softer voices. Emphasis can come by the contrast between a normal tone of voice and either softer tones or rougher tones.

The speed of your voice is also important. Reading slowly brings emphasis, especially when you punctuate the words with short pauses and stronger timbre. Slow reading can also convey slow thinking or slow movement by a character in the story. Fast reading can convey fewer important details, or quick movements and thoughts. Smaller variations help keep the story interesting. Don't be afraid to pause occasionally, if there is something worth reflecting on for a moment.

You can add to most any story an occasional comment such as, "Hmm . . . I wonder what he was thinking," or "What do you think will happen next?" or even, "Do you think that was right?" A bit of interaction during the story helps the child whose mind is wandering to reengage with the story line. Of course, all this assumes the story is written in an interesting manner; choose your Bible storybooks with care. We are amazed how dull some of those books we loved as children are now, but other available books are written in a more interesting, creative manner yet are faithful to the content of the Bible.

You may also want to practice your facial movements when telling a story. Children may look at the pictures in the book, and if they know how to read, they may follow along with the words. But every now and then, or perhaps even more often, they will look at your face to see your expression and how involved you really are in the telling. When my daughter and I watched *The Lion King* professionally acted on stage, I was impressed that even the puppeteer—who walked around the stage holding Zazu the bird—used facial expressions to convey emotions.

If you have preschool children, you may want them to do some movements during the story, to keep them involved.[1] For example, you might begin a telling of Jacob's dream of the stairway by having the kids rub their eyes, yawn, lie down, and close their eyes. Similarly, when someone in a story gets hungry you might have the kids rub their tummies and pretend to be hungry. When good things happen in the story, children can be encouraged to smile and clap their hands; when bad things happen they might be told to say, "No, no!" as they shake their heads. If you include these activities during a story, they will encourage the kids to stay involved. These are not as appropriate for older children, who will see them as childish. Instead they may like the idea of your changing hats as you change characters in the story or of using chalk or markers to draw a picture of the story as you tell it (more on drawing later in this chapter).

While this next point is probably obvious, make sure the child is comfortable and focused during the telling of the story. If the mind is on something else before the story begins, it may be good to talk for a minute or two about that, so that the child will be able to focus on the story. If children are forced to hear a story they don't enjoy, you may be inadvertently communicating that the Bible is an unpleasant book. On the other hand, if you put your arm around your child and hold her close, that warmth and affection can also be associated with the Bible

1. VonSeggen and VonSeggen, "Puppets and Presentations that Connect with Kids," 127–29.

story. Those emotional associations are at least as important as the content of the story.

With practice, you can become a great storyteller. You might even mention to your child that you are learning how to do it, and they might even tell you how you are doing! Don't be afraid to depart from strictly reading the words, if need be. Sometimes you may need to ask the child questions. Sometimes the story bogs down into irrelevant details that need to be skipped if you see your child becoming bored. There may even be a time when you realize an important detail is missing and you can add that as well. It is a good idea to read the account in the Bible prior to reading the Bible story so you will be more sensitized to the elaborations, omissions, and mistakes that a story may have. Listen to good storytellers such as Garrison Keillor on public radio stations, who tells the stories on *A Prairie Home Companion*,[2] or Frank Peretti's audio stories.

Be sure to vary the kind of story used according to the age and ability of your child. Short stories with more pictures are appropriate for younger children; longer stories with fewer pictures are good for older children. Even after they can read for themselves, kids often like to have stories read to them. Even at age twelve, our daughter still asked us to read to her once in a while; it is a wonderful time in which to connect with your youngster.

There are also times to tell stories from your own experience, such as when you became a Christian or of other spiritual experiences you have had. Your kids may also be interested in stories from your childhood, or of how you met your spouse. These help give them an identity that is distinct. Not every story needs to have specific biblical content; children also need to be exposed to some of the classic fairy tales and even some of the ancient Greek stories, because they are a part of our Western cultural heritage. You may prefer for them to hear these on the television if your storytelling time is extremely limited, or you may prefer to read them so you can comment on principles that fit with Scripture or differ from the Bible.

Don't be afraid to spend money on good Bible storybooks. We own a set of fifty small books that have only one story each, that are great for preschoolers and early elementary-level children. Sometimes the better books are not more expensive, so look carefully before you buy a whole

2. While this program is on many public radio stations, you can also hear it on the Internet at http://www.prairiehome.org.

set. You may also want to purchase some cardboard or paper posters for your stories and lessons.[3]

Enacting Bible Stories

A step beyond the Bible story is to act out a story with your children.[4] While you can do this with one child, it is usually more enjoyable to have more than one child participate. You can serve as the reader or teller and the negotiator or guide, at least initially, but we encourage you to consider taking a role in the drama as well. If the lead role is complicated, it may be good for an adult to take that role the first time through so the children will be able to imitate your example.

This is probably not a good idea for bedtime stories, because the activity may actually make the child more alert and make it harder for the child to go to sleep, although it might work if done an hour or more before bedtime. Playing out a story could also be a weekly event or saved for special times of the year (such as during the biblical holidays—see chapter 9).

Enactment or "story play" has been researched by educators and found to be very helpful in many ways, and the evidence suggests that it may be the most effective way of teaching stories up to second grade, and at least equal to other methods after that point.[5] The research also indicates that enacting stories in the home context is more likely to result in better performance of the story, probably because the child will be less inhibited and comfortable in that setting than in others. Enacting stories is associated with better comprehension of the story, increases in social cooperation, and possibly intelligence-test scores.

3. We put together a series of lessons on the Ten Commandments that included biblical stories, other stories we made up, and other activities. We used ten large cardboard posters with drawings on them that we found at a Christian bookstore. The drawings listed the commandments and had cartoon characters drawn on them to illustrate each commandment. Unfortunately the commandments were written in King James English, but that didn't matter too much because we taught them to preschoolers, who couldn't read. We simplified some of the commandments. The cartoon characters on the charts were very helpful and we created our stories involving those characters.

4. A good example of this practice is available at http://www.childfaith.net.

5. I summarize much of the literature on this subject in Ratcliff, "Stories, Enactment, and Play," 247–69.

It can be helpful to add props (objects used in the drama), but you can also encourage your children to imagine those objects. Midway between pure imagination and a prop would be to use one object to represent another (a pencil might be considered Moses's rod, for example). Older preschoolers can begin to imagine at least some objects, while older children can imagine more and even describe some of the details to imagine that you might forget!

You do not need a script, although you may want to jot down a few notes reflecting the major events in the story. You might even want to get a small chalkboard on which you write a word or two for each major event, just to be sure you get the chronology correct. It is good to play out a story several times, changing roles with each retelling. You might even include some of the neighbor children, if their parents approve; this could be a good way to witness to unbelievers or help disciple the children of fellow believers. But things may be difficult if you have more than five or six children involved, or if the children are very different in age. (Trying to match a less complicated yet active role with younger children may help overcome this problem.)

You may want to provide just the main story line, or you may want to add some commentary. (Don't get carried away with the latter.) Be sure to give plenty of speaking and acting parts to the children, even if that takes some elaboration of the basic content of the story. On the other hand, try to give roles that the child can understand and from which they can learn. In the process, the child gets into the story, becomes a part of the story, and thus learns not just the content of the story but also a simulated firsthand experience of it. With this comes an emotional involvement that will perhaps help them feel like the character in the Bible.[6]

Selecting stories with action is important. We suspect the story of Job would probably be better read than acted. On the other hand, Joseph's story in the Old Testament (Genesis 37, 39–47) could be acted out in several phases; indeed researchers have found that enactment in phases is more likely to help children in recalling the story later, especially with preschoolers. We have read that the journey from home to Egypt was most likely walked over a period of several weeks; thus one can imagine how hot, tired, and thirsty Joseph must have been as the slave traders took him to be sold to Potiphar (Genesis 37). If possible, derive the

6. LeFever, *Creative Teaching Methods*, 90.

added details of the story from good commentaries or other books about the Bible so as to be faithful to the story context as well as content.

You can also have your older children enact an interview with a biblical character.[7] You might even suggest this prior to telling the story, so your kids will pay close attention. You will probably need to help them with some of the answers, but this is an effective way to help them get inside the key biblical figures. They may even want to pretend they are Larry King or a news anchor doing the interview; fourth through sixth graders love imitating singers, movie stars, or even the president! Just imagine Arnold Schwarzenegger interviewing Paul about his shipwreck! Make it even more interesting by recording the drama with a video camera, and then play it back for the family.

Of course, not all Bible content is appropriate for enactment or even reading. For example, the bloody account of Jael's murder of Sisera (Judges 4) or the rape of Tamar (2 Samuel 13) should be reserved for the teen years, in our opinion. As mentioned earlier, consider the child's abilities and age in choosing stories. It is also important not to sanitize a story a great deal; it is easy to idealize favorite characters and not bring in the sometimes rough and difficult details that the Bible includes, such as Jonah's depression and anger after the people of Nineveh repent.[8]

Enacting Applications, Role Playing, and Family Puppets

Enactment can be used not only to tell Bible stories, but also to simulate real-life applications of biblical principles. For example, a skit on one child's sharing toys with another could be enacted as an application of the account of the early church having everything in common (Acts 2). Children can learn a Bible story or study a passage but easily overlook or forget possible applications. Through enactment children can play out applications you suggest. Another possibility is that you can give your child a situation to act, and let him or her come up with applications of a Bible passage along with the action.[9]

7. VonSeggen and VonSeggen, "Puppets and Presentations that Connect with Kids," 132.

8. While I have rarely seen this part of the story included in Bible stories, I admire the *Veggie Tales* story of Jonah for including this element.

9. This is technically termed "inductive learning"; see LeFever, *Creative Teaching Methods*, 87.

Should such enactments be prescribed for children, or should we allow applications to emerge more spontaneously? We think it is good to let children reflect upon the story, suggest possible applications, and then briefly enact one or more applications. However, this is more likely to happen with older children than with younger kids. It may also be that younger children will not connect the story and the application due to less mature levels of thinking. Yet we must avoid underestimating youngsters, and so we can ask how they might apply the story personally, or just listen when they offer applications more spontaneously. We suggest, however, that you think of some possible applications of the story in advance and have the children enact those, especially if they do not come up with any on their own. And we are certainly not saying that applications need to be enacted every time; children may need time to process the implications of stories, and they might suggest very relevant applications several hours or days later. Enactment of any kind may be most effective when it is an occasional treat rather than a routine duty.

It is also possible to teach children some of their roles at home or church using enactment. I (Don) helped preschoolers learn and refine several church roles using enactment.[10] Holding short worship services led by children can be interesting for the children and can be a method of learning as well. You could also have your child role-play sharing their faith with other children in school or other places, given that role play helps children try out a new role in a protected environment. It is often a good idea to follow role-playing or most any enactment with a discussion so you can see what has been learned and what may have been missed. It is often valuable to repeat role-plays until they are effective and accurate, and participants' switching roles between enactments can be helpful.[11]

Enactment is somewhat different from Jerome Berryman's *Godly Play* (see chapter 4) and sometimes different from our celebrating the biblical holidays (chapter 8). Godly play requires a special physical context because of the requirement of quietness and reflection, and involves moving physical objects as the child reflects upon the story. The goal is facilitating not only reflection but also the possible experience of God.

10. Specifically, the roles of preaching, collecting the offering, praying in church, and leading the singing. The children who replayed their roles learned much faster and better than did another group of children who received verbal correction. See my article, "The Use of Play in Christian Education," 26–33.

11. LeFever, *Creative Teaching Methods*, 88, 90, 102.

Enactment is more likely to be a lively activity, especially if more than one child is involved, and thus quiet reflecting is less likely during the enactment, although certainly the child might reflect quietly later on in the day. It is possible that children could have a spiritual experience while acting out a story, but the goal of the activity is more that of experiencing what the biblical characters experienced and comprehending the story more completely. Understanding and the physical experience of biblical characters does not rule out having a spiritual experience as well, but such experience is more likely to be incidental rather than the main purpose. Enactment also tends to be a more social and interactive procedure, with room for fun and laughter, whereas this is probably less likely during a Godly Play session.[12] Certainly the methods and goals of the two procedures complement one another, and we think it might be possible to use both approaches albeit in different locations.

Enactment can certainly be added to the activities involved in celebrating the biblical holidays. Children are active during many of the activities recommended in chapter 8, but it is more likely that they will do and say things that fit into a somewhat more ritualistic context. For example, they will eat a bitter herb (horseradish) celebrating Passover to symbolically understand the harsh conditions of slavery in Egypt. But before or after the Passover Seder, there is no reason children could not enact some of the events of Passover. Again, the two approaches can be complementary.

Puppets can be a welcome addition to telling Bible stories or playing out applications. They are easy to use and can quickly capture the attention of younger children. Using a puppet can be as simple as moving the mouth in time to a song about your Bible story played on a tape or CD. Older children may be interested in using the puppets themselves to enact or role-play. It is crucial that your children be involved, either taking turns using the puppets or having dialogue with the puppet. While researchers have discovered that enactment is the most effective way to teach stories to preschoolers, using puppets is only slightly less effective, discussions are somewhat less effective than puppets, and then in order of decreasing effectiveness are drawing, retelling the story, and finally being told to pay attention. You might try using several methods, or at

---

12. It should be noted, however, that Jerome Berryman in *Godly Play* speaks of laughter possibly accompanying spiritual experience.

least changing your methods regularly; using the same approach every time will probably make that method get old very quickly.

Some guidelines for using puppets might be considered.[13] You should open and close the mouth for every syllable, not for every word, and make sure the eyes look at your kids. You don't need a stage, but if you want one, you might use a table turned on its side or a blanket draped over a rope hung between two objects inside or outside the house. Preschoolers especially like fluffy, soft puppets, and actions will be more important than words. At this age it may be best for the puppet to only require yes or no responses from the kids. Preschoolers can also be encouraged to sing along with puppets, or clap in time with the music. During the early elementary years the puppet might answer children's questions about a Bible story, but they are especially good for telling Bible stories and talking about the lessons from stories. Older children may like to play games with the puppet, such as the puppet's answering yes-no questions from children as they try to guess what Bible character the puppet represents. School-age children can make puppets and even present the Bible story as a puppet show for younger kids or neighborhood children. Using sound effects can be very helpful with puppets as well as in storytelling and enactment.

A Wide Variety of Methods to Consider

While we are especially appreciative of Bible stories and enacting those stories because of their strong research support, there are dozens of other possible ways to help communicate the message of a Bible passage to your children. We will be relying upon two books that are actually written for church ministry for children.[14] From these sources we will draw ideas that would be doable in the home with one to four children. If you have more children than that, or want to include some of the neighbor

13. VonSeggen and VonSeggen, "Puppets and Presentations That Connect with Kids," 122–25.

14. LeFever's *Creative Teaching Methods* is especially helpful, and she includes several chapters on the issue of how to push yourself to be more creative in working with children. Every chapter has something that a parent can use with a child, but many of the ideas primarily apply teenagers. (Still, there are a number of good illustrations for children.) A second good resource is Jutila et al., *Children's Ministry That Works!*, although most of the chapters relate primarily to church situations. I draw from four of the twenty-two chapters in my comments.

children, we encourage you to get the original books for more ideas that fit a larger group. You may want to look at the original books to fill out the descriptions and find examples as well. We encourage you to pick and choose those methods that fit the personality and interests of you and your child, but don't be afraid to try something unfamiliar to you or your youngster. The worst you can do is not to do it well, and that may provide a wonderful time of laughing for everyone involved. Consider including your spouse as well!

The Old Standby: Bible Memorization

Memorizing Bible verses is something that has been with us for a long, long time. Early in the Old Testament God says, "These commandments that I give you today are to be upon your hearts. Impress them on your children" (Deut 6:6). There is an entire book on helping children memorize Scripture,[15] and we encourage you to use some of those methods. It is indeed impressive to hear children recite lengthy Scriptures, and many children can memorize quickly and easily during the school-age years. As teenagers, they may be able to use that knowledge in Bible quizzing.

Yet don't overlook the next verse after the above command: "Impress them on your children. Talk about them when you sit at home and when you walk along the road, when you lie down and when you get up" (Deut 6:7). That the passage teaches us to talk about the commandments suggests that the verses chosen are meaningful to the child. We encourage you to choose Scriptures that are understandable to children—parroting words that are not understood may lead to later parroting of theology, songs, or Scriptures that one does not believe or at least does not think about. Be sure to use a modern translation with appropriate vocabulary for a child, and be sure they understand and can apply what the memorized Scriptures say. Try not to convey the idea that more memorization is the same thing as stronger spirituality.

Mime for Me and My Kids

Mime is distinctive from enactment in that no words are used, and thus it calls upon more imagination from the child whether she is doing mime

15. See Susan Lingo's *Written on Our Hearts.*

or watching another child (or parent!) doing mime.[16] Children can be wonderful mimes. As suggestions, we encourage you to make sure mime will actually teach something that relates to the Bible story, either an application or the story itself. It is also helpful to not give your children a lot of time to prepare to be a mime; they tend to be more spontaneous if only given a few minutes to decide how to do a mime event. Traditionally mimes may act out either male or female roles, regardless of the sex of the mime. Discussion following the mime experience is usually helpful in making sure your children get the key points.

Playing Games

Games appeal to children of all ages, but children are most likely to follow the rules consistently after about age six or so. Competitive games have a specific goal, and kids try to reach that goal before the others. When your children are very different in age, competitive games may not be as enjoyable, although we found that our teenage sons enjoyed such games with our preteen daughter. Sometimes the competitiveness can interfere with getting the main point of a Bible story, as losers feel disappointed and winners may become a bit proud! But I (Don) must admit I enjoy playing *Bible Trivia*, perhaps because I once beat a seminary professor at the game!

Here are some pointers for developing games that relate to Bible lessons.[17] First, make sure you know the main idea of the lesson and make this the focus of the game. Second, it is best if you can think of a game that your children already know how to play, and adapt it to the Bible story you are studying. Third, after playing the game, discuss what your children learned in the process. Finally, be sure the game fits the abilities and ages of the children: two- and three-year-olds need games that involve a lot of movement and not coordination with other people; four- and five-year-olds enjoy running, jumping, and other more precise movements, as well as games that involve pretending and games with other children, so long as there are not a lot of rules; six- to eight-year-olds enjoy games that involve both broad and fine movements, more complex directions, and games that involve chanting and rhymes; and

16. LeFever, *Creative Teaching Methods*, 108–33.

17. Vermillion, "Great Games for Kids," 93–102.

nine- to twelve-year-olds can play games with more complicated rules, that involve teams, and that have an obvious ending.

Noncompetitive games are sometimes called simulations, and involve simplifying some aspect of the real world to promote increased understanding.[18] For example, World Vision has a simulation in which youngsters go thirty hours without eating anything and only drinking some juice. The point of this simulation is to try to experience what it is like for the many thousands of children and adults in the world who go to bed hungry each night. Of course it does not give them the full experience, because they know that after the thirty hours they will again eat, but it does simulate the experience of chronic hunger to some extent.

Flannel Is Not Just for Underwear: Illustrating, Retelling, and Discussing a Story

Do you remember the old flannel-graph board and paper figures of Joseph and his brothers that stuck to the board? Some of us remember Sunday-school teachers who used those things every Sunday when we were kids. They are still around, and you can make your own flannel graph inexpensively by simply covering a sturdy piece of cardboard with flannel and taping it on the back of the cardboard. Asking around at church may net you loads of flannel-graph figures: teachers often throw them away after using them, but sometimes they get packed away in a storage room. And once you've got them, don't be content with just using the figures to tell the story; let your kids use the figures to tell you the story as well.

Encouraging children to retell the Bible story—either by using the flannel graph or just by talking—is not only a good way to evaluate how well they remember the story, it also tells you something of how they are interpreting it. Providing prompts if the child forgets a section is a good idea but be careful that the child does not begin to think that the forgetting is wrong. You might encourage your youngster to "ham it up" a bit, adding a few creative details, so long as the retelling does not become silly and frivolous.

18. LeFever, *Creative Teaching Methods*, 134–71.

While we have mentioned discussion as a follow-up to other methods, it can be considered a method in its own right.[19] Discussion is good because it helps the child review and make clear the basic point of a Bible story. Sometimes when they are trying to apply a Bible story, discussion can help kids find the solutions to their difficulties. Discussion can stimulate children to creatively apply what they have learned. They may also hear more mature perspectives that may nudge them toward increased spiritual maturity. Views on the topic of a Bible story may be strengthened as they defend or explain their beliefs and opinions. This stronger conviction may also make them more likely to tell other children about their views. A variation on discussions is to have an interview, which we mentioned earlier.

Making a Case for Case Studies

A case study is a brief summary of an actual experience.[20] Older children can create case studies from Bible stories, or the stories may already be considered case studies. Possible applications of a principle from a Bible story might also take the form of a case study. Older children can be given a case study of King Solomon, for example, and then asked what the positive and negative qualities of the king were. If you develop a case study of an application, such as something that happened to a friend at work that relates to a Bible story principle, it is a good idea to change the name and details. Case studies that are applications should be similar enough to what your children experience for them to make the connection.

The advantage of case studies is that they help children develop their ability to make decisions, they expose children to opinions other than what they hold, and they may result in greater tolerance for minor differences between people. If you decide to use a case study with your older children, be sure you get all of the important facts, try to anticipate specific details that might come up in the discussion, be sure to have a specific purpose in using the case study, and develop some questions that will help begin the discussion. In addition to the Bible, some good sources for case studies are people you know, your own experiences, Christian and secular magazines, newspapers, and history.

19. Ibid., 202–16.
20. Ibid., 217–35.

Creative Writing for the Creator

Writing or journaling is another teaching method that can be used with your older children.[21] Younger kids might benefit by your journaling for them their key insights and experiences that relate to principles from Bible studies. The first time you do this with your children, make it fun: write about a church trip to an amusement park, for instance. Encourage your kids to not think of this activity as like a school assignment, but rather to consider that writing is the same thing as talking—except that it is written. Sometimes it helps for children to briefly write down their ideas or applications about a Bible story—before they discuss it with you or others. Ignore punctuation or spelling errors; to mention these makes you too much like a schoolteacher and the writing like a school assignment. Use writing with Bible stories that will help children solidify their beliefs about God, people, and the Bible. You might want to provide a spiral ring notebook so there is an ongoing record of their thoughts about the Bible, of decisions made, and of applications as the result of studying a Bible story—a record that they will want to keep for years to come. This writing has the advantage of helping your child become more creative in thinking, and if some details from writings are shared with brothers and sisters, you may find that one of your children can more effectively preach to the others than you would ever be able to do! It is also helpful for you to keep record of insights and applications your children discuss related to Bible stories, noting the spiritual growth of your children. You may also find that existing writings and poetry related to Bible stories are also of interest to your children, if the reading level fits their age level.

You may also want to consider having your children write out some prayers that incorporate ideas from Bible stories, but it is best to respect their privacy if they do not want to share their prayers out loud with you or with other children. I have found that my writing out prayers can push me to apply the Bible to my own life. Encourage your children to use common, everyday language in written prayers and encourage them to honestly describe their feelings about the Bible story or related applications. Written prayers should be specific, and can include promises to God.

21. Ibid., 236–59.

Other kinds of writing assignments for your children might include paraphrases of Bible content. When I (Don) was a child, I once began to paraphrase the whole Bible. (I think I got to Genesis chapter 3!) I also recall rewriting the book of Amos so it involved a modern church pastor. Another possibility is for children to write letters to missionaries or to their children, to senior citizens, to people in the military, to those who do not get much appreciation for their work in the church, or to individuals who have lost a loved one. Incorporate portions of Scripture or ideas from the Bible in the writing. One last idea for writing assignments is to take the perspective of a biblical character and to write from that viewpoint about what happened in a Bible story. For example, your child could write a diary entry from the viewpoint of the girl Jesus brought back from the dead: one entry might reflect what happened just before she died, and then another entry might reflect details just after she became alive again. Another example would be to write an account of the crucifixion of Christ from the perspective of a bystander or as the reporter for a newspaper.

Music for the Master

Music is yet another avenue for teaching about the Bible and for helping children personalize the message of a story.[22] Younger children enjoy clapping their hands, playing percussion instruments, making hand movements, and changing facial expressions in time to music that you play on the piano, another instrument, or the CD or tape player. As with choosing Bible storybooks, in selecting music be sure the message of a song is biblical; indeed you might make an assignment for older children to find a biblical basis for a song. Older children may enjoy listening to or performing music, but you might also challenge them to write a song: have them take a well-known tune and write words that go with your Bible story of the day. They might also be willing to create a tune for a psalm or other passage of Scripture.

Music is best used after your children hear the Bible story, as it tends to punctuate the main idea or ideas in the story.[23] Carefully evaluate the words for age appropriateness: simple songs with repeated phrases are

22. Ibid., 260–68.

23. The ideas in this paragraph are primarily from Hopkins, "How to Lead Music with Kids," 114–20.

best with younger children, while older children may be better able to understand ideas that are more abstract. Sometimes children have a strong preference for a particular style of music, although some experimenting with older styles may be valuable as well. If you are teaching a new song, begin by teaching the chorus and then teach the rest in short segments. In addition, do not teach more than one song during a session unless the tunes are familiar and your children are older.

Artwork: Drawings, Pictures, and Crafts

Children of all ages generally like to draw, and we encourage you to have your children draw pictures that relate to a given Bible story. The story itself or a modern application could be the subject of a drawing. Original art can reflect a great deal about the child's feelings and reactions to a Bible story.[24] Children might also go through catalogs and magazines, cutting out pictures to form a collage or mixture of original art and pictures.

Another possibility to introduce a drawing activity is to ask children to carefully choose colors for drawing.[25] For example you might ask your older youngster to choose a color to represent the feelings of a person in the story, and then draw the person using that color. Then they could choose another person in the story with different feelings and use a different color to represent that person's feelings. Or the same character might be drawn with different colors reflecting various parts of the story. Then discuss with them why they chose the colors they did and what feelings those colors represent. They could also draw themselves and the feelings they have about the story or certain characters in the story.

Another helpful art project for older children would be to draw pictures representing different sections of the Bible: history, poetry, prophets, gospels, New Testament history and letters, and finally Revelation. Different biblical sections as well as separate biblical situations or people might each get a separate color.

24. Robert Coles's excellent video *Listening to Children* illustrates his use of children's drawings to understand their lives and perspectives better, including their spiritual views and experiences. He encourages *them* to interpret their own drawings.

25. Most of the ideas on art from this point on come from LeFever, *Creative Teaching Methods*, 269–90.

Children can use poster board, watercolors, paint, chalk, pencils, crayons, and even clay and paper to make art projects that relate to Bible stories. They may even want to make a giant illustrated Bible storybook, and use it to tell Bible stories to their friends and younger brothers and sisters. The content of artwork can be symbolic or very literal renditions of a Bible story. Some children may even want to try cartooning a Bible story or application. Photography can be used to capture applications of a Bible story in today's world.[26]

Crafts are a form of art that has been associated with children in churches for many decades. A story from the Bible can be reinforced by the child's building a craft. This can be another way children can "get into" a story. Some guidelines for adult supervisors include providing sufficient time to complete the craft, securing a sufficient and appropriate amount of space for the work, preparing in advance (it may be hard for your kids to patiently wait as you read instructions or obtain materials), having water nearby, ensuring that children wash their hands and cover their clothing, keeping electrical appliances out of the area, encouraging creativity, and complementing the progress of your children.[27]

To encourage your children in making crafts, it is good to have plenty of materials available, including paper, various writing implements, paints, scissors, tape, paste, and glue. Children of different ages are likely to prefer different kinds of crafts, and the kinds of crafts are only limited by your imagination, but be sure the craft relates to what you want your children to remember about the story or an application of the story.

Work by well-known artists throughout history might be used to illustrate Bible stories. If several paintings or drawings of the same biblical event can be found, it is possible to compare how different generations looked at those biblical accounts. (This may have the added bonus of helping children to develop art appreciation.) Some modern art reflects feelings of doubt and emptiness; these too might be reflected upon, using key biblical passages that are helpful alternatives to those portrayals. Libraries, museums, bookstores, and the Internet are possible sources for such artwork.

26. A Christian school in Hawaii even gave children cameras to try to capture images in the children's experiences that reflected Christianity. The results became a beautiful book that helped save the school from bankruptcy. See Mecum et al., *God's Photo Album.*

27. The ideas in the paragraphs on crafts are largely taken from Swan, "Adventurous Art and Creative Crafts," 103–13.

What Page Are You On? Using the Internet

Learning about Bible stories may also involve use of the Internet.[28] Stories and applications can be summarized on Web pages, with the help of parents. (Some advanced older children may be able to create Web pages for themselves and their younger brothers and sisters.) Many recent word processors can create Web pages with little more than entering a single command, and very often if you have any kind of Internet service you will also be given Web space for a Web page. Free space is also available on the Web.[29] A variation of this idea is to make Web pages for a favorite missionary—with their permission, of course. While this would involve obtaining information about the country, about the language spoken there, about the backgrounds of the missionaries and their families, about needs, goals, and the like, the Bible might be included as part of conveying information about the work on the mission field.

When our daughter became concerned about friends who were reading books related to witchcraft, she made a Web page that discussed the problems with the books and explained why witchcraft was wrong. She linked this special page to her Neopets Web page, which her friends visited almost every day. She avoided the embarrassment of direct confrontation yet made her views clear in the process.

E-mail may be used for dialogue between older children about Bible stories and applications. It might even be an evangelistic tool in which key biblical passages are used to witness to others. Of course you need to monitor such dialogue carefully; the person receiving your child's e-mail could be uninformed about Christianity, a member of a cult, or even a pedophile. It is important both with e-mail to strangers and public Web pages not to give any personally identifying information, particularly

28. While many of the ideas in this section are my own, I credit LeFever, *Creative Teaching Methods*, 291–305, for prompting my consideration of this medium, and also for some of the ideas included here.

29. One danger of using free space is that advertisements may pop up when someone looks at your page, and those ads may be for gambling or even pornography (a pop-up blocker may help, but some pages are able to bypass the block in some manner). At least one Christian site offers free Web space, but sometimes even Christian sites compromise on the kinds of ads permitted, especially gambling advertisements. Facebook pages could also be created for this purpose, but the high standards for advertizing that were once affirmed by this group have been significantly compromised. It should be noted that many Web page systems that are commercial-free are not expensive and can be very user friendly.

addresses, phone numbers, birthdays, or even last names or one's general location.

The Internet can also be used as an information-gathering device for ideas related to a Bible story or passage. Again, this needs to be carefully monitored, given the large amount of worthless information and doubtful sources that might accidentally be taken too seriously. The Internet also poses the threats of pornography and time-wasting or overcommercialized Web sites.

Dance to the Music

Our daughter at age two listened to a videotape titled *Kids Sing Praise* dozens and dozens of times. The video was little more than a group of children singing lively songs, but it was her favorite video. She loved it and would occasionally dance about the room as she watched the program.

Some of us grew up in homes where dancing was strictly prohibited. Any movement in church was suspect, other than the waving arms of the song leader, the ushers' seating people, or passing the offering plate. Today we have many churches with all kinds of movement in the congregation and on the platform. Some of these churches are wonderfully alive, and a few go to excess. We may each have our personal opinions about the degree of physical movement that should take place in church, and some of us still restrict our children when it comes to social dancing, but two-year-olds and lots of movement just seem like a natural combination.

So let your children express themselves in movement and song. The Bible tells us that David was so excited about the ark of the covenant that he leaped and danced before the Lord with all of his energy as the procession moved to Jerusalem (2 Sam 6:14–16). Likewise, Moses's sister, Miriam, danced with a tambourine, singing a song of victory after the Israelites crossed the Red Sea on dry ground (Exod 15:20). We too should rejoice in all that God has done for us, and in his personal relationship with us. We must not be like David's wife Michal who criticized his free expression before the Lord (2 Sam 6:16). Yes, there are times to be serious and reflective before the Lord, but exuberant praise and worship are also very biblical. Experiences with God can take a wide variety of forms across a very broad spectrum from quiet to loud, inactive to very active. And if you are little daring, you might consider joining your kids in the joyous celebration!

Conclusion

If you feel a bit overwhelmed by hearing about all these methods of teaching and applying the Bible, don't feel bad! Just choose the one that sounds the most interesting and doable and give it a try. If it doesn't work, or if you just want more variety, try another. You have several years to try them out, and of course you can just avoid those that have no interest at all for you. Many of these you may only want to use once a month or less often.

In whatever way we teach our children, we must remember that we are not preparing them for a test, but for a relationship. Whether we have them play games to understand the Bible better, or if we have them visit a sheep farm to understand Jesus as the Good Shepherd, we need to help kids reflect upon possible applications but also let the Holy Spirit develop the parallels within the child, so they experience the "aha!" of discovery. We need to emphasize that there is another possible level of experiencing a Bible story, in which the child personalizes the story as being a message from God to the child. God speaks to children through the Bible, although he can speak in other ways too. Let your youngsters personalize biblical truth in their own time and their own way, as directed by God. Let them have the freedom to express that relationship with Christ and faith in God in their own distinctive ways.

| SEVEN | # Daily and Weekly
              Rhythms of Faith
              Children's Rituals

> *"If anyone does not provide for his relatives, and especially for his immediate family, he has denied the faith and is worse than an unbeliever."*
> *(1 Tim 5:8)*

THIS POWERFUL VERSE IS found within a lengthy passage on relationships with elderly people and younger people in the church. However, the verses that immediately precede this verse relate to people in one's literal family, and specifically widows who are faithful believers. A few verses later, younger widows are encouraged to marry, have children, and manage their homes. Thus it may be reasonable to extend this verse to the care of children, as well as widows. The underlying principle is just what appears when the verse is read without the context: caring for the immediate family, including the children, is a crucial test of whether a person is really a Christian.

Looking at this passage in context, we note that this provision clearly includes physical care. But we are particularly impressed with the contrast between the godly widow of verses 9 and 10, with her "good deeds," and the unspiritual widow who "lives for pleasure" and is considered dead (5:6). We believe the striking contrast between a godly person and one who is pleasure oriented reflects that provision is more than merely physical care. Throughout the Old Testament (which most of the New Testament Christians knew well), spiritual care was extremely important, as we have noted in previous chapters (see Deut 6:6–9). The spiritual training was to take place while sitting, walking, lying down, and rising in the morning. Faith is central to everyday life within the family, not just for Sunday or church. We know that children are more likely to adopt the faith of their parents (perhaps with some fine-tuning of applications for the new generation) if faith is part of daily life, as such a faith gives meaning and purpose for all of life.

Tasty Rituals—No Boredom, Please!

In chapter 7 we mentioned the possibility of an evening bedtime story and prayer each day, as well as periodic special activities related to the Bible. Here we want to explore more closely the daily and weekly activities of a spiritual nature that you may want to consider in your own family life.

Several decades ago it was popular to talk about the "family altar," which did not refer to a literal physical altar but rather to a time of Bible reading and prayer among Christian families, whether before the children went to school in the morning, at the dinner table, or sometime in the evening. It was a wonderful idea in theory, but as noted in the previous chapter, it could be very tedious. The best thing we remember about the "family altar" was when it ended and we could finally get back to something interesting.

We think it is a shame to bore children. Proverbs 22:6 states, "Train a child in the way he should go, and when he is old he will not turn from it." We are told that the word "train" has the connotation of a mother cow licking her calf's lips to give it a taste for milk.[1] This picture is much more compelling for teaching our children God's ways and God's Word, and contrasts vividly with my experience of the "family altar," although we have met some people who have had a much more positive experience of this practice than we did.

Some of the Old Testament practices emphasized traditions and rituals that can often be very interesting to children, and can be presented in a manner that points to Jesus in the New Testament. These can with the right preparation fulfill what was intended with the "family altar;" making faith a part of daily and weekly family living. In the next chapter we will extend the application to the yearly spiritual holidays as described in the Old and New Testaments.

1. Dobbins, "Too Much Too Soon."

Healthy Families Have Rituals

One study of five hundred teachers, pastors, counselors, and other professionals found fifteen characteristics of healthy families.[2] Two especially stand out that relate to this chapter: enjoying traditions as a family and sharing one's faith. A worthy goal for Christian families is to combine these—sharing our faith as a family by enjoying traditions.

Having traditions in the home makes members of the family feel a part of something bigger than themselves and produces a feeling of belonging.[3] They symbolize the family and reinforce the values of the family by "putting clothes on" those values. Jewish people have a strong cultural and religious identity in part because of their traditions and rituals, and especially the rituals and traditions practiced in the home.[4] The presence of such practices brings predictability to family life, so that no matter what else may happen, some things will always occur.

The second through fifth books of the Bible were difficult for me (Don) to appreciate during the first thirty plus years of my life. All the details of the tabernacle, all the sacrifices, and so many other aspects of these books seemed entirely irrelevant to modern life. Then I tried something new in my devotions; I decided to read Deuteronomy first, then retrace my steps by examining the first three books. Not only did I find the content of Deuteronomy more interesting, but it dawned on me what was a key theme that unlocked the riches God has in these biblical books: the theme of traditions and rituals. Obviously these are very important to God, otherwise he would not have given us so much detail to them in these books. It was in part the traditions—as well as the wilderness experiences—that helped provide the Israelites with a sense of community.[5] As someone once said, "Traditions put flesh on our theology and values," reaching beyond the here and now to what is ultimate and transcends daily experience.[6]

2. Curran, *Traits of a Healthy Family*.

3. Gaede, *Belonging*.

4. Campolo and Ratcliff, "Activist Youth Ministry."

5. Technically speaking, a strong sense of distinctive corporate identity did not emerge until after the time of the judges and the beginning of the monarchy. However, tribal community becomes strong through the traditions and common experiences, and later the traditions helped encourage a sense of ethnic distinctiveness, as they do to this day among Jews.

6. These understandings are found in both Curran's and Gaede's books, and the examples that follow represent Curran's ideas as well as a few of my own.

Close-knit families have traditions such as

- taking a Sunday afternoon walk;

- looking at picture albums;

- opening Christmas presents on Christmas eve (or Christmas morning);

- baking and eating Christmas cookies and sweets;

- bringing in the Christmas tree, decorating it on Thanksgiving afternoon (or on the first day of Advent), taking down the tree on New Year's Eve;

- celebrating birthday parties, and eating your favorite food on your birthday;

- designating story- and prayer time before bed;

- celebrating Easter by wearing new clothes to church, by dyeing and hunting for eggs;

- telling stories of family members, including of the family's "black sheep";[7]

- designating Wednesday or some other night as the night for eating leftovers for super.

I (Don)] vividly recall my father's regular practice of cooking pancakes on Saturday mornings. While my father rarely cooked at any other time, this was a strong tradition for several years in my family of origin. I looked forward to Saturday mornings, but I hated the rest of the day because of the "tradition" of my cleaning the garage!

You may want to take a few moments to reflect upon those traditions and rituals that were important to your family when you grew up. Ask yourself, which of these have you, or will you, include in your present family; which will you discard, and are there additional rituals that you would like to add to your family life? Just a word of caution—it is easier to continue a tradition you grew up with or that has emerged in your current family life, than it is to begin a new tradition.[8] Traditions

---

7. I do not intend any racial implication by using this term; there simply is no adequate equivalent way of describing those family members that "go bad" and are examples of what children should *not* be. Such negative examples are very instructive by showing what is devalued in the family, and by implication what *is* valued.

8. Gaede, *Belonging*.

are precious, and because of the difficulty beginning new ones, be careful not to discard too quickly.

Children Naturally Have Rituals

One of the things that surprised me (Don) the most about my research with children in a public school was the many rituals in the hallway. Some of these rituals were imposed by teachers, such as standing or walking in line. But especially when teachers were not present, children took part in a wide variety of rituals, such as rubbing the walls with their hands or body, jumping to reach the top of the frame of doors, dancing routines, and many other rituals.[9] I found that these occurred almost continually in the hallway when a teacher was not present, and sometimes even with a teacher present.

The fact that children manifested such rituals, usually without encouragement from teachers or peers, suggests that rituals are deeply ingrained into the human race. Rituals are important because they connect to what is meaningful for the child. We are not convinced that children consciously realize how important rituals are, but the fact they are so common in their lives (as well as in the lives of adults) implies that they are very important. But I must admit that sometimes I wonder, "Do children engage in rituals merely because they are bored?" Perhaps. But they could do other things to pass the time, such as talking quietly or just waiting for a teacher to return. But usually they go into another mode of acting in the hallway and in many other places as well—a mode where repeated actions predominate, activities that may reflect a transcendence or meaning beyond the person.

Adults are ritualistic as well. We tend to have routines that frame our getting ready for work in the morning and bedtime rituals that make us ready for sleep, for instance. Even secularists find much meaning in such everyday rituals.[10]

9. See my "Rituals in a School Hallway," 9–26. Also see a very similar version of the research, under the same title in the Education Resource Information Center (ERIC) database.

10. Of the many books on this subject, one of the more easily read is Imber-Black and Roberts, *Rituals for Our Times*. For an interesting Christian perspective, consider Pottebaum's *The Rites of People*. Pottebaum is Roman Catholic, but his ideas fit many Protestant evangelical contexts equally well.

Daily and Weekly Faith Rituals

In a sense you can consider the bedtime Bible story and prayer for your child to be a ritual. Having prayer before or after eating a meal is also a ritual. Regularly listening to a particular television program can be a ritual. While children have many rituals related to getting ready for school in the morning, going through the day at school, and getting ready for bed in the evening, we will focus here on daily rituals related to the Christian faith.

We realize many families these days do not have what we see as routine: the bedtime prayer and Bible story. Yet these are easily combined with other rituals the child may have for going to bed, and thus if you have a regular bedtime for your child, it may blend in better and thus be practiced more faithfully. Even as our children approached their teen years, they regularly reminded us of the need for prayer, kisses and hugs, and other aspects of "being tucked in." It was as if the day could not be complete without those bedtime rituals.

Another part of that daily routine, although it could be done at the dinner table or at another time, is what has been termed "the God hunt."[11] The child and parent together look for evidence that God was at work in the activities of the day. Too often we do not reflect sufficiently on what God is doing, and thus we do not see him at work.

We enjoy the 2002 science-fiction movie *Signs*. It tells the story of Graham Hess, an erstwhile Episcopal priest who has become an agnostic upon his wife's sudden death, but whose faith and calling return after he helps repel an alien invasion in order to rescue his son, Morgan, from being captured. We enjoy *Signs* because viewers (eventually) can see God at work in the film, even in the tragedy of the automobile accident that takes the life of Graham's wife, Colleen. Glasses of water that their daughter, Bo, "thoughtlessly" leaves around the house are discovered to be the best way to combat the aliens. God graciously allows Morgan to have asthma so that his life is spared. God is everywhere, even though we don't see how this can be possible until late in the movie. Ultimately the entire movie reveals how God uses everything to draw the wayward minister back into fellowship with him. We need to reflect more on how God is at work in our lives, seeing his hand in events that may at first glance seem to be accidents.

11. Mains, *Making Sunday Special*, 43–44. For a fuller consideration of this topic, see Mains, *The God Hunt*.

In order to be aware of God's work in your own lives, you could keep a journal together with your child, noting prayer requests, answers to prayer, and other evidences of God's activity. Some families may find this wears out quickly and thus may only add to the journal once a week. In our family we did it sporadically, every few months, looking back at the big picture of how God had answered prayers and moved in our lives. This is a practice we encourage you to consider, at least two or three times a year, if not more often.

Some parents may want to add another element to the evening meal or bedtime preparations: blessing your children.[12] This involves pronouncing a statement of some desirable future over your children. It does not have to be formal, or even planned in detail. For example, you may choose one night to say, "Sweetheart, I wish for you a happy marriage to a wonderful boy, and that you will stay pure until you are married." On another night you might say, "Son, I ask God that he will help you know what areas in your life can be used for God—whether in your job, in your church, or in other places." Again, some families prefer to do this once a week as part of a special weekly celebration, or just occasionally—every few weeks. In my family this ritual was occasional, and sometimes we would include close friends, who would then bless their children; or we might swap kids and would bless each other's children. If the children requested to do so, they would also bless their parents!

A ritual you might want to consider is to set aside a day for all-day worship. Throughout the day you might wear something special such as a large cross or a special garment that will remind you to praise God, thank him, sing to him, and to do similar activities regularly throughout the day. Encourage your children to do the same. Some may be able to do this two or three days a week, while for others it might be only one day a week or just an occasional practice. A somewhat-similar practice would be to set aside a special day for pushing yourself to infuse faith into everything that happens. Remind yourself—tie a string around your finger if you need to—that God is at work in every area of life, and pause every few minutes to think of how the current activity reflects his work in your life. As you do this, describe what you are thinking to your child and encourage her to try to think in this way as well. We suspect these kinds of all-day activities will be better for early elementary children,

---

12. Two very fine sources on this topic are Hayford, *Blessing Your Children*; and Smalley and Trent, *The Gift of the Blessing*.

but some children might want to try this for themselves during the later childhood years.

When we discussed Jerome Berryman's Godly Play approach in an earlier chapter, we mentioned that you might want set aside a special place in your house devoted to special times of worship and reflection. It might be a corner of the basement or even a chair in the backyard. Interestingly, in the nineteenth century people often set aside such a "sacred" space in their homes.[13] You might want to encourage your children to visit that special place once a day, or perhaps once or twice a week; perhaps encourage them to write in a journal as they reflect for a few minutes. This is not a practice for every family and every child, but it is worth considering.

The Old Testament emphasizes the importance of the Sabbath— the practice of setting aside a special day each week for prayer, Bible reading, and reflection. While keeping the Sabbath is one of the Ten Commandments (Exod 20:8–11; Deut 5:12–15), many Christians no longer follow this practice other than by going to church on Sunday. Actually the Apostle Paul may have addressed this issue in the New Testament when he said, "One man considers one day more sacred than another; another man considers every day alike. Each one should be fully convinced in his own mind" (Rom 14:5). We say that Paul *perhaps* addressed the issue of Sabbath keeping, because some hold that Paul is talking about annual holidays from the Old Testament, and still others believe he is speaking about both the Sabbath and holidays.[14] Regardless of Paul's specific cultural context, the principle of periodic rest and change from normal patterns of behavior is an important one.

We think that many of us Christians, perhaps most of us, need to rediscover the Sabbath and make one day a week special in our turning away from regular work and turning toward reflecting and worshiping. We don't think we need to be legalistic about this, although many of us are impressed with Eric Liddell's costly decision to observe the Sunday Sabbath, seen in the movie *Chariots of Fire*. But the principle of taking

13. The idea of the family having a special, sacred place for worship is mentioned in Marjorie Thompson's *Family: The Forming Center*, 24. The chapter emphasizes the centrality of the family and home in the worship of the 1800s; indeed the family is described as the "Domestic Church." For a somewhat similar analysis that sees the nineteenth-century home as the place for the integration of worship, education, and domestic life, see McDannell, "Creating the Christian Home," 187–219.

14. Arrington and Stronstad, *Life in the Spirit New Testament Commentary*, 780.

one day of comparative rest is a good one. We think this day could be a Sunday, a Saturday, or perhaps even parts of two days a week sometimes. One day of seven being given primarily to spiritual concerns may be a tradition that will help us live the rest of the week in light of what we discover from God on that special day.[15]

For many years when our children were younger, we often set aside Saturday evening as a special time to prepare for Sunday. In this way we followed the practice of Jews both in biblical times and in our own time, except that the Jewish Sabbath (*Shabbat*) begins on Friday evening, and the Sabbath day is Saturday. The goal of our familial practice was that as a family we would attempt to have all the preparation for Sunday church attendance completed prior to sundown (chores done, baths taken, clothes laid out for church—including shoes). The special evening began each Saturday as I (Brenda) lit candles and recited the traditional blessing, in English rather than Hebrew: "Blessed is He and blessed be His Name." I then covered my eyes and continued: "Blessed are you, Lord our God, King of the Universe, who has sanctified us with His commandments, and commanded us to light the Shabbat candles."[16] Sometimes this would be followed by a blessing over bread or drink. (We preferred tea to the fruit of the vine.)

Then we ate together, sometimes just as our family and sometimes with another family—either with close friends or with someone who wanted to experience a Christian *Shabbat*. Following the meal I blessed the children (or they blessed me). Afterward we sometimes would have a blessing of the spouse while reading and personalizing a portion of Proverbs 31, or occasionally we had a "God hunt" (see above) or some other celebration. We believe it was meaningful for everyone in the family because it created space in our busy lives for rest, for reconnection with each other and with God, and for a more tranquil start to Sunday morning.

In our study of the Sabbath, we found a number of parallels between the account and words of Jesus in the gospels and aspects of the Sabbath observance.[17] For example, the Old Testament Sabbath command to rest

15 The Mainses' books are excellent resources on this matter.

16. Adapted from Kasdan, *God's Appointed Times*, 3.

17. Brenda has developed a detailed curriculum that includes observing the Sabbath as well as celebrating the biblical holidays. It is available without cost at the following Web site: http://www.brenda.ratcliffs.net/roots.htm.

is paralleled by Christ's comment, "Come unto me, all you who are weary and burdened, and I will give you rest" (Matt 11:28), and the lighting of candles recalls his statement that "I am the light of the world. Whoever follows me will never walk in darkness, but will have the light of life" (John 8:12).

You may or may not want to try observing the Sabbath, beginning what we consider the evening before the special day. Perhaps you will place some restrictions on family activities for one day a week.[18] This may fit some personalities and schedules better than others. What is most important, we think, is that there is a special time set aside, preferably every week, when you and your children give God the center of attention, and have family rituals that are meaningful to you and your kids.

---

18. Again, beware of being legalistic in this respect; you may obtain obedience through harsh enforcement of rules yet lose the heart of the child. If the child grows up and rebels against arbitrary rules, you may have lost the child's heart and soul. Even if the child becomes equally legalistic, it may be at the cost of his having a close relationship with our Creator. Legalism is a "slippery slope"—rules can lead to more rules, until there is little or nothing more to one's faith.

| EIGHT | # Touching, Smelling, and Eating
The Biblical Holidays

ABOUT THIRTY YEARS AGO we saw *Fiddler on the Roof* for the first time. The movie made a deep impression on both of us as it reso-nated with our study of the Old Testament Israelites. We did not know much about Jewish people, but that movie made us want to learn more about Judaism, the Sabbath, and eventually even Jewish weddings.

I (Don) grew up in the home of parents who met in Bible school: my mother came from a pastor's home, and my father entered the min-istry shortly after they were married. Yet in spite of the their teaching me richly through Bible stories and my attending church since infancy, I knew almost nothing about the holidays until I read some of Chaim Potok's novels.[1] While I didn't care for Potok's theology, I deeply appreci-ated his characters and the way most of them honored their faith and the traditions they celebrated.

My (Brenda's) parents were both missionaries, and my father also has served as a pastor for many years. In spite of my strong background learning about the Bible and the Christian faith, as well as four years of Bible college, I also knew little about the rich legacy of Jewish tradi-tions and rituals—a legacy that is ours as "grafted-in" people of God (Romans 11).

We were impressed that Tevye, the main character in *Fiddler on the Roof*, and millions of Jews like him saw the Sabbath observance and the celebration of the biblical holidays to be not only obedience to God's

---

1. His best-known novel is *The Chosen*. Most of his novels are vivid accounts about Jewish people who struggled with maintaining or adjusting their theology to fit modern life. During his lifetime Potok was often invited to speak to Christian groups about his novels and Judaism. He passed away in 2002.

commands but also a source of identity and self-preservation. While you can see ethnic and cultural aspects in some of the ways the feasts are celebrated by Jews today, in many respects the yearly observances are still similar to what has taken place for hundreds and even thousands of years. Jesus probably celebrated them similarly (in some ways) as Jews do today. Jewish heritage and history are reflected in these annual celebrations, connecting them to a long line of biblical ancestors and history.

In our churches, we usually celebrate Christmas and Easter in special ways. Some churches go further and celebrate Advent and Lent. Special activities may surround even the Fourth of July and perhaps other special days as well. But it is unusual to find a church that takes seriously the holidays described in the Bible, celebrating and honoring those days in a special manner. This seems so odd to us; we have special days of celebration, but we usually neglect the days that the Bible tells us to celebrate.

We are certainly not against celebrating the holidays distinctively linked to the Christian faith, and even celebrating national holidays is fine. Indeed we especially enjoy Thanksgiving Day because it reflects some themes of the Feast of Tabernacles that occurs just a few weeks prior to Thanksgiving. The Pilgrims may even have had this in mind at the first Thanksgiving. And we always celebrate Christmas, with a focus upon the children's enjoyment of the day and their understanding what the day represents—honoring the birth of our Lord. On Easter we look forward to the message of the angel at the tomb, and our kids—when they were small—participated in the annual Easter-egg hunt each year with their friends. These are all well and good.

We are not legalistic about celebrating the biblical holidays, because the Bible clearly says, "One man considers one day more sacred than another; another man considers every day alike. Each one should be fully convinced in his own mind. He who regards one day as special, does so to the Lord" (Rom 14:5–6a). This may apply to observing the Old Testament Sabbath or to the annual holidays, or some take it to only apply to the monthly lunar cycle celebration. Regardless of how one reads Romans 14:5–6a, it is clearly not a prohibition against celebrating certain holidays, but an appeal to tolerance on the issue.

Celebrating these holidays can be an instructive experience in which children learn not only about the events of the exodus, but also what those events mean to Jews and for Christians today. Not only do children learn from the activities, but spiritual experiences may possibly occur as they participate in the activities. Being physically involved in the celebrations helps them "get inside" the Bible stories. The ceremony, the beautiful candles, the personal involvement, and all the special preparations allow for the possibility that youngsters may experience God during these celebrations.

The Seven Feasts Plus Two

We have found that celebrating the biblical holidays, as well as occasionally celebrating the Sabbath (albeit on Saturday evening instead of with the original Friday-evening meal) has been very meaningful to our children and to us. We have adapted them a bit to fit our situation, especially emphasizing aspects that reflect qualities of the life and work of Christ. A number of sources available today explore what we consider latent Christian implications in each of the biblical feasts, which makes them for us more distinctively Christian celebrations. We also include some of the Jewish rituals that fit well with our faith.[2] We shorten some activities, such as the Passover Seder, retaining the aspects that have the most meaning for children, and that involve them in some kind of physical or verbal activity. We have even been invited to lead Seders in several churches, highlighting their Christian aspects yet honoring the Jewish roots to the Christian faith. To do so seems like a completion of our faith, given that even a casual reading of the New Testament reveals that Jesus was very Jewish.

The seven biblical feasts are most fully described in Leviticus 23, although other passages provide additional details about one or more of the feasts. Four of these (Passover, Unleavened Bread, Firstfruits, and Pentecost or Weeks) occur in the spring, and the other three—the Feast of Trumpets (Rosh Hashanah), the Day of Atonement (Yom Kippur),

2. One source we found especially helpful as we began to explore this topic was Zimmerman, *Celebrating Biblical Feasts in Your Home or Church.* Also see Kasdan, *God's Appointed Times,* rev. ed., and Kasdan, *God's Appointed Customs.* Brenda's Webpage on the holidays—notes from a thirteen-week seminar that has been presented at several churches—can be accessed at http://www.brenda.ratcliffs.net. For those who want to explore this area in depth with their children—even learning Hebrew in the process—consider an extensive, multiyear curriculum (with forty-plus volumes!) written primarily by Jeff and Pat Feinberg. Jeff is a Messianic rabbi who leads a congregation in the Chicago area. Check his Web page at http://www.flamefoundation.org for details.

and the Feast of Tabernacles (Booths)—occur in the fall. In addition, the book of Esther prescribes an eighth feast (Purim), and the ninth is mentioned in the New Testament as a feast Christ celebrated (John 10:22): the Feast of Dedication. This is now called Hanukkah; it celebrates a miracle that is believed to have occurred in the period of time between the Old and New Testaments.

It is a very effective way of learning, and the Bible in essence prescribes this method with the statement that the feasts be celebrated every year and that they involve children (Exod 12:24–27; 13:3–10). From the moment of birth, children learn best by touching and manipulating objects. Even in the elementary-school years, holding and moving objects (termed "manipulatives") help children understand and learn more quickly. This is one reason why approaches to spiritual formation that foster a child's active involvement with tangible objects can foster spiritual experience, as seen in Jerome Berryman's Godly Play approach. It is very instructive to note how the feasts involve children in various activities, and most of the events are expected to take place at home, led by the parents. By repeating these celebrations each year, children hear the words again and perform the activities again; understanding grows a bit more each time. Educators call this approach the "spiral curriculum," which involves teaching a particular lesson several times, spaced months or even years apart, but each time drawing the child to a more advanced level of learning. Layer by layer, understanding grows and develops with each observance of the holiday. Again, a new and effective educational method used widely today is foreshadowed in the Bible.

We can be sure that Jesus celebrated these holidays as a child, as did most if not all of the New Testament writers. Thus as we explore and celebrate these holidays, they can help us gain a stronger understanding of the background that the writers of the New Testament, and many of the early Christians, shared, and reflected in their writings and worship. To leave these days unexamined is to miss some of the meaning of what is written in the New Testament as well as the flavor of the New Testament church while it was still very influenced by the Jewish backgrounds of Jesus, Paul, and the majority of the leaders and people who made up the earliest church.

While a full consideration of how families can celebrate each of the biblical holidays is beyond the scope of this book, the remainder of this chapter will concentrate upon children's activities in the celebration of each of the nine holidays. Some holidays call for greater involvement than others, and most of the activities suggested for children are as much or more from Jewish tradition than from the biblical accounts. We have added a few ideas of our own to the traditional rituals. Yet the Jewish people have celebrated these traditions in an effort to honor and obey the prime directive in teaching children (Deut 6:7). Please bear in mind we are not suggesting these are required of Christian parents. Rather, they are suggestions you may want to consider. We believe that the freedom we have in Christ indicates that such ceremonies and rituals can be creatively added to, omitted, or adapted as you sense God's direction so that they best fit your family and the personalities of children and parents. Many of them can also be shared with other families in a home or church context. For additional details on the Christian implications of the holidays and rituals, as well as fuller descriptions of the specific activities, consult Brenda's Web page or other fine sources on this topic.[3]

Children's Activities during the Feasts

Passover is, without question, one of the most important feasts in the Old Testament. Over and over it is mentioned as the event that shaped the beginning of the people of Israel as a distinctive group. The centerpiece of the celebration is the Passover Seder, a group of activities and readings as family members sit around the table, and in the middle of the celebration, the family enjoys a meal.

The youngest child who can read is given the task of asking three central questions, to which the parent replies with different parts of the story of the exodus from Egypt. The youngsters take part in sprinkling single drops of juice onto a saucer, representing each of the plagues experienced by the Egyptians. Four cups of juice are drunk by the children and adults, representing sanctification (being set apart from other people), the plagues, redemption from Egyptian bondage, and praise. At the serving of the third cup (the cup of redemption), Jesus broke the bread and passed the drink to his disciples at the Last Supper, and so we often have a family communion service at this point in our meal. All present consume the unleavened bread called matzo (much like crackers), as the

3. http://www.brenda.ratcliffs.net.

appearance of the bread is compared to Christ, our "living bread" (John 6:51). During the Passover Seder the matzo is hidden (*buried* is the term often used), just as Christ was buried; and then the children scramble around the house to find the hidden bread. Adults and kids eat several different foods, including horseradish, which represents the bitterness of slavery. All the foods in this meal represent something about the exodus and also may imply something about Jesus.

The second biblical holiday is the Feast of Unleavened Bread, which actually begins the day after Passover.[4] While traditional Jewish families do a "search for leaven" before Passover begins, at the start of Unleavened Bread may be a good time for you to consider performing this ritual with your children. The house is thoroughly cleaned in the Jewish household so that no leaven (yeast or products made with yeast) can be found anywhere in the house. Leaven symbolizes sin. The children make a systematic search for some bit of leaven that might have been overlooked in the cleaning process. Usually parents leave a tiny mound of crumbs in some remote area of the house for the children to brush into a little bag. The child who finds the crumbs may be applauded or perhaps given a small reward. You may want to leave a few crumbs in several places so that each child has something to find. The end of the ceremony involves burning the leaven, and then all take a moment to search for hidden sin in their own lives in order to give this to God in prayer.

The third feast is Firstfruits: the first Sunday after Passover or the last day of Passover if it is Sunday. This day often coincides with Easter Sunday, and Jesus rose from the dead on the Feast of Firstfruits. Paul commented, "Christ has indeed been raised from the dead, the firstfruits of those who have fallen asleep" (1 Cor 15:20). You and your children may want to purchase some fruit, especially fruit just beginning to ripen at that time of the year in your area. These fruits can be offered to God either by giving them away to someone who needs them or by dedicating them to God before you eat them. You may want to celebrate the resurrection of Christ by watching a movie about his life. My (Don's) favorite is the clay animation video *The Miracle Maker*. Another possible way to celebrate the resurrection is to get some old family photographs of people who have gone to be with the Lord and to talk about how they will some day rise from the dead, just as Jesus did.

4. The terms "Passover" and "Unleavened Bread" are used interchangeably in the New Testament.

Fifty days after the Feast of Firstfruits is what the Old Testament calls the Feast of Weeks and what the New Testament terms Pentecost. In biblical times this was a pilgrimage feast during which all men were to travel to Jerusalem for the celebration. You may want to plan your own pilgrimage by having a hiking trip to a favorite spot or by traveling to a place that has special spiritual significance for you and your children. Another possible way of marking Pentecost is to celebrate the birthday of the church, described in Acts 2, which occurred on the Day of Pentecost. A birthday cake might be appropriate, as would a special offering for the church. Since the Jews consider this to be the day that God gave the law on Mount Sinai, it might be appropriate to celebrate the birthday of ancient Israel or to include such a celebration with the celebration of the church's birthday. You might include an emphasis of how the church was grafted into the vine (Romans 11), which represents Israel. The evening before the Feast of Weeks, Jews have a custom of studying the Torah (the first five books of the Bible) all night. This might be a good time to have a sleepover at your house and perhaps to watch movies such as *The Prince of Egypt* or *The Ten Commandments* and then to recite the Ten Commandments at midnight. Since this is also considered a time to be kind and charitable, it might be good for you and your child to volunteer for a soup kitchen or other social outreach agency for the day.

The Feast of Weeks is followed by the Feast of Trumpets, or Rosh Hashanah. Curiously the Bible does not give much instruction about this day other than the command to blow the trumpets. You might consider the purchase of an actual ram's horn (a small one usually costs less than fifty dollars). Blowing the ram's horn is not easy, but anyone who plays a brass instrument can probably make some sound with it. Jews today celebrate the civil new year with this feast, and if you are up to a second New Year's celebration, go for it! Just as the Feasts of Passover, Unleavened Bread, and Firstfruits reflect Christ's crucifixion, burial, and resurrection, and just as Pentecost is the birthday of the church, so some believe that the Feast of Trumpets reflects the second coming of Christ. Indeed, there are many parallels between traditions surrounding Rosh Hashanah and Christian understandings of Christ's return. You may want to discuss the return of Christ, and even take your children to a cemetery to talk about how the dead will rise first, and that then we will join them (1 Thess 4:16–17). But be careful; this might be frightening to younger children. A more traditional ceremony for Rosh Hashanah is called the Tashlikh. It involves going to a river or lake. Everyone in the family reflects silently for a few minutes on sins that need to be confessed to God. All then confess their sins silently as each person throws pieces of bread, small stones, or pocket lint into the body of water: The objects thrown represent each sin confessed. In this process, the sins are "buried in the deepest sea, and remembered no more" (Mic 7:18–20). The overall Christian emphasis of the Feast of Trumpets is on being prepared for the second coming of Christ.

The Day of Atonement, or Yom Kippur, comes ten days after the Feast of Trumpets and is considered the most holy of all the biblical holidays. It was the one time of the year when the high priest entered the Holy of Holies to obtain forgiveness for the people of Israel (Leviticus 16). You may want to observe a fast or partial fast with your children for the day—a traditional activity at this time. If you have a special place in your home set aside for teaching or Godly Play, as mentioned in an earlier chapter, you may want to plan some extra special activities there for this day. Perhaps you may want your children to act out some of the things the high priest did so that they see how difficult it was to obtain forgiveness from God. Then you can point out that Jesus now is our high priest, and his death provided our forgiveness of our sins; we no longer must make animal sacrifices. You might even reenact the tearing of the curtain in the temple, which gives us free access to the most holy place with God.

Five days later comes the last of the seven holidays in Leviticus: the Feast of Tabernacles. To celebrate this holiday a small Sukkoth or booth ("tabernacle") is customarily built, usually attached to another building. It can be made of tree limbs and rough lumber, and should be rather flimsy and very temporary.[5] The booth reminded the Jewish people of their ancestors' staying in tents or booths while wandering in the wilderness. Building such a booth is not difficult if you have trees nearby and can find some broken limbs to make the booth. Use ropes rather than nails to hold it together. Let each of your children play a part in the construction of the booth, so they discern what is involved and will feel it is theirs as well. According to the biblical account and Jewish tradition, for the seven days of the feast, families were expected to live in the booth, eating their meals, sleeping, and spending much of their time

---

5. Written by Stephen Eastman, instructions for building a Sukkoth, including drawings of the construction, are available at http://www.ratcliffs.net/eastman/taberna.htm.

there (Lev 23:41–42; Deut 16:13–15). You may be content to eat just a meal or two there, or perhaps to sleep there in sleeping bags with your children. Hopefully they will be grateful to live in the house again after sleeping out a night or two. (At least you will be!)

The last two feasts, Hanukkah and Purim, were added on to the seven in Leviticus prior to the time of Christ, and generally occur in December and February respectively. Two special events in the history of the Jews are celebrated at these times. Hanukkah honors the account of an oil lamp that burned well beyond the expected amount of time, as recorded in the books of Maccabees in the Apocrypha. You may want to downplay the idea of a miracle, as this is in a book that many Christians do not consider part of God's word. Indeed, even Jews sometimes note that there would not be as much interest in celebrating this holiday if it didn't fall during the same month as Christmas! Jesus did go to a ceremony that honored Hanukkah (John 10:22). The day is marked by playing family games, giving and receiving presents, eating special foods (such as potato pancakes), and lighting candles.

Purim is great fun, especially for younger children. It is celebrated by reading aloud the story of Esther (or perhaps an abbreviated version), and every time the name of Haman is uttered during the story, the children are to make noises with their feet or with noisemakers. It is a rowdy, festive celebration and can be compared with Mardi Gras. Giving gifts to the poor is a common activity on this day, as are eating special foods and wearing costumes.

We have provided a brief overview of biblical holy days in this chapter. Since we first became interested in this topic, many wonderful resources have been published to help inform and guide Christian families who desire to incorporate this part of our faith history into their family's religious life. It is easy to become overwhelmed when you begin to study this area. But if you begin the process of learning about the holidays, each year you too will experience a deeper understanding of the spiritual truths that each of these days represent: you can learn and grow with your children through these observances.

| NINE | # Communion or Commotion
Children, Parents, and the Church

T HE CHURCH IS AN important resource for your child, as some earliest impressions of God are formed in that building and by the people in that building. Going to church and worshiping God are virtually synonymous for many children and indeed for quite a few adults as well. Many people date their conversion from an experience in the church. Dropping the kids off at church will not be enough to keep them in the faith; how can an hour or two a week prepare a child for the other 166 or 167 hours? The church should not be the only place children learn about and experience their faith, but it can be a helpful resource supporting parents in their task of spiritually training their children. Research indicates that it is the accuracy with which children understand their parents' beliefs, and the encouragement of activities related to those beliefs—such as attending church—that predict whether children will adopt those beliefs for themselves.[1]

It is in the church that children come to know believers linked primarily because of belief rather than because of friendships or family.[2] The result of this linkage is that children are likely to understand God's work as it is defined and lived out by the local church. Attending church is important, but it is equally important to attend a church that loves and affirms children regularly and overtly, not just when there is a Christmas pageant.

1. Okagaki, et al., "Socialization of Religious Beliefs," 273–94. It should be noted that young adults at the time of the study reported adopting parents' beliefs—a reflection of the impact of parental beliefs during childhood.

2. Having lived in the Deep South, I realize that there are some small churches that are sometimes referred to as "family churches" because most everyone who attends is related in some way to the others. I served as the interim pastor of one such church, and I appreciate having had the experience.

Preparing Children for Church: More Than Just Clothes

It is easy to get into the habit of sleeping in on Sunday morning, then frantically trying to get the children ready for church as you are getting ready. This can cause quarrels and conflicts, which put everyone in a sour mood and make folks less than receptive to what the pastor may have to share. Conflict can also keep you from hearing what God wants to communicate to you through a teacher, the pastor, or the music that is sung. Who feels like worshiping when just moments ago you had to discipline a dawdling kid?

In contrast to this scenario, it is possible to prepare for Sunday the night before. This fits with the fact that the Old Testament believers saw the day as beginning at sunset, and thus the Sabbath began on Friday night. In our *Shabbat* observances (which we held on Saturday nights), before the Saturday evening meal, the children were to take baths, lay out clothing, find shoes, and do all the other things needed for Sunday. During the meal we used our best dishes and spread the table with a fine tablecloth. We welcomed God's gift to us with the special meal: his Sabbath. A fringe benefit of this habit was that our children could learn how to act at a more formal occasion, a skill that will be beneficial for the rest of their lives. The net result was not that every Sunday morning before church was perfect, but this preparation did help us all focus on the importance of the special day before us.

Give some thought to how to prepare children for church. Some families may find that an evening of preparation is not workable because of schedules and other problems. If this is the case, you might consider an unusual beginning of the day on Sunday. Try having a special breakfast, early enough that the children (and you!) can leisurely enjoy the meal before getting ready for church. Another possibility is to make a special breakfast the result of getting ready by a designated time; say, if everyone is ready for church by 8:30, you will stop by a pancake house and still be able to get to church by 9:30.

We think the time after church can be as detrimental as the struggle before church. Some have quipped about "having the pastor for lunch" (finding fault with the sermon during the meal). While there is certainly a place for critique (we are told in scripture to be discerning), it may be more beneficial to discuss what was gained in church as you eat your noon meal after church. If the children join you in church, you might ask them to talk about the subject of the message, and older children may even be asked what Scriptures were used and about the main points made. Given that this could become a laborious task, perhaps some special treat could be offered for correct answers.

Sunday afternoon could also be a special time for children and parents. When I (Don) was a child, one of my best friends was forbidden to play any games or even to watch television on Sunday; instead he was required to read the Bible and pray. As a result, he developed a rather negative attitude toward the Christian faith. Today I am not even sure he professes to be a Christian. His parents meant well, as they took very seriously the commandment to observe the Sabbath. But all he thought of was the fun he was missing because his family insisted on such rules.

If you want your children to do special things of a spiritual nature on Sunday afternoon, make them enjoyable and rewarding. And be realistic about what is appropriate for children; they may learn more about God by your reading a Bible story at night than by your restricting them from baseball on Sunday.[3] Perhaps they will even learn a lesson or two about ethics and morality in a baseball game, as well as get needed exercise.

Worshiping Together or Apart?

We have often heard the question, what would Jesus do? Indeed asking this question became a fad for a number of years among Christian teenagers, and it is a good question that can help us make some of life's more common, everyday decisions. But let me ask you a variation of this question: What would Jesus do if he attended your church this week? Would he sit quietly and listen, like most everyone else, or would he be asked to say something or even minister to the congregation? Would he even be invited to read the Scripture for the day, as he often did in the synagogue in the first century?

Luke 9:48 equates welcoming a child with welcoming Jesus. In a sense, the child acts as a proxy for Jesus. So how well does your church welcome our proxies for Jesus? Does your church welcome children? Do they provide a place of ministry for children or even allow them to read

3. Yet I realize that people differ on this matter. I admire the strict adherence to Sabbath keeping of Eric Liddell in the movie *Chariots of Fire*, but it was an inner conviction that he followed, not something that was imposed upon him from without. He also did not try to impose his convictions on others.

the Scripture aloud in church? We think it is important that children attend services that have something to say to them. However, if a church service has little or nothing to offer children, then we question whether their attendance is appropriate. Many churches have alternative activities for children during Sunday-morning worship, on Sunday evenings, during the midweek evening service, or at other times. These can be beneficial if they are led by creative, gifted teachers who love the Lord and love children. We encourage you to go to class with your child if they feel comfortable with that. If your kids would rather you not attend with them, perhaps you can stand outside the door or in some other inconspicuous place to hear what takes place. We believe it is very important that you know what your child is experiencing in church, even if it means asking the church to add a microphone and camera to the room where children are taught. A good church wants to know what children are being taught and how they are taught.

On the other hand, we think a church should have at least occasional intergenerational services. This does not mean just adding children to a standard church service. Rather, the intergenerational service purposefully includes children, involves children, and gives children content appropriate to their age levels. Children can take part by enacting stories, singing songs, and participating in other activities. How much more interesting—for both kids and adults—it would be to punctuate a sermon with such engaging activities than to give a standard sermon that misses most children and even some adults. We may need to rethink the traditional sermon if we are serious about including children in the church service. What would Jesus do? What do we do to Jesus in the form of his proxy, the child?

Diversity in Worship Styles

One of the things we hope you will do with your child is encounter a wide variety of worship styles. Not all of us feel completely comfortable with every worship style, to be sure. But we believe it can be instructive for children to be aware of many styles of worship that exist. It may be that you will want to take a few Sundays to visit different kinds of churches (perhaps when you are on vacation) so that children can experience this diversity. Even watching television broadcasts of church services can be broadening, as long as we encourage kids not to make fun of approaches with which they are not familiar.

For example, some churches have a massive pipe organ that accompanies the stately old hymns sung by the congregation and professional choirs who enter the sanctuary in a processional to begin the service. Others churches have drum sets that may even be used to punctuate a sermon, and those attending may dance in the aisles. Some churches have moments of silence in the solemnity of the sanctuary, while other churches have such loud singing that the neighbors complain. We personally appreciate cathedrals with statuary, stained glass, and pastors in beautiful vestments. We have also enjoyed the lively service of a storefront church on the Caribbean island of Antigua. Children need to see the diversity of the body of Christ so they will be more accepting of Christians from across the spectrum of worship styles.

In the Bible we see a similar degree of variation in worship, from the "wheel within a wheel" of Ezekiel's vision (Ezekiel 1) to the God of the thunderstorm in Psalms (e.g., Psalm 29) and the breathtaking throne of God in John the Revelator's vision (Rev 20:11–15). In contrast is the "still, small voice" of God (1 Kgs 19:11–12) and the silence of the wilderness experienced by Moses (Exod 3:4–6), Jesus (Mark 1:9), and Paul (Acts 9, 22). We enjoy and appreciate many ways of worshipping, and children can benefit from experiencing such variety, seeing God as bigger than any one worship style and approach. Too often children get the idea that there is only one way to worship, which is quite different from the biblical record.

Can Children Minister to Adults?

As we think of the opportunities a local church has in helping and nourishing children, we must ask what kind of ministry the church should have with children. Many churches believe that their task is to entertain children, and the goal is that children come to prefer church activities over television. (TV is a tough competitor!) Other church "ministries" see themselves as babysitters, taking care of the kids while the parents are in church. Still other churches see children's ministry as that of teaching, which is better than mere entertainment or babysitting but still reflects a one-directional effort. Another possibility is that church can be not only a place where children learn, but also where children can minister to others. For too long we have forgotten about the fellow believers in Christ that almost every church has, but who are often overlooked as actual ministers: the children. If we believe children are genuine believers, then they should have an area of ministry.

I (Don) spoke before an audience of children when I was eleven or twelve years old. My family was visiting an uncle, pastor of a medium-sized church, and they were having a vacation Bible school series that week. My uncle asked me to give my testimony at the church before 150 to 200 kids at the VBS. It was an exciting experience, one that I will never forget, because finally I realized I could actually do ministry! I suspect I was also pretty scared, but I will never forget the confidence the pastor—my uncle—had in me. What would Jesus do? What do we ask Jesus—in his proxies, our children—to do in church?

Children need to learn how to minister to other children. But they can also minister to adults. Now this won't happen overnight, but it is a possible goal. Children can learn to pray, give praise, sing, and even tell what God is doing in their lives. The rest of the believers present—children and adults—can benefit and even learn from children. Of course we will need to have some tolerance for mistakes, and ways of gently correcting youngsters. Children will need training and practice before they publicly begin to minister. Children, like adults, have different gifts, and not every child has the gifts that fit public ministry, but she may have the gifts that fit private ministry. We need to discover the gifts God has given our children and make use of them. One of the keys to making intergenerational ministry work effectively is to activate ministry by children to their peers and adults as well. Most churches come closest to this idea when children are asked to minister on a missions trip or at a nursing home. These can both be valuable experiences for children. But we should also equip youngsters so they can minister in our church services as well. Their "equipment" needs to include their knowledge about ministering and about their spiritual gifts, their discernment about whether a desire to minister is from a clean heart or tainted by pride or the desire for power; and of course our equipping children must include fostering the ability to sense God's leading in ministry contexts. Children can be a vital resource to any church! Open the door to the ministry of Jesus—through our children.

Spiritual Mentors

Spiritual mentors are people gifted by God to encourage and nurture less mature believers. Usually we think of one adult mentoring another adult, teaching the basics of the faith, the spiritual disciplines such as fasting, prayer, retreat, and the like, and also encouraging a strong walk with the Lord. Children no less than adults also need mentors. Sometimes a Sunday-school teacher may take on this function, but no teacher is likely to be able to meet individually with each of her, say, twenty children during the week!

However, as children get older, it may be a good idea to look for a mature adult who can become a mentor. Senior citizens may become "grandparents" that "adopt" your children as "grandchildren," or older couples may "adopt" younger couples and their children.[4] Ideally, the mentor has been carefully screened by the church, including a police check and general background check. It is unfortunate but true that there are adults who would lead children into sin under the guise of being a mentor. Jesus's words about having a millstone around the neck and being thrown into the sea for leading a child into sin (Luke 17:2) are not just a warning for those who could harm children emotionally, physically, or spiritually. It is also a warning for parents to beware of adults, teenagers, and older children who might harm the child.[5]

But there probably will be a time, most likely in early to middle adolescence, when children will not hear your words as well as they once did. If your child has developed a healthy relationship with a mentor, she may talk with the mentor even if she does not share concerns with you. In a sense, mentorship in late childhood can be a faith hedge for adolescents: you can choose, or help to choose, an individual whom the

4. Stonehouse, *Joining Children on the Spiritual Journey*, 39–40.

5. The reports of sexual abuse by priests may be one reason why clergy ratings were at an all-time low at the time of this writing; see Religion News Service. "Clergy Ratings at Lowest Point Ever." This is not just a Roman Catholic problem; predators look for any context where they have access to children without much supervision, so this can be a problem for any church—and particularly for churches that do not have careful screening policies for volunteers who work with children. More recently the film *All God's Children* has revealed this problem in at least a few missionary boarding schools. Compassion Ministries president and CEO Wess Stafford also mentions this in his book, *Too Small to Ignore*. Perhaps the best policy against abuse would be to place video cameras in every classroom with children, and perhaps in preschool restrooms as well.

young person will respect and listen to when advice and other kinds of help are needed.

A Christian Bar Mitzvah?

Paul Meier suggests that we consider some special rite of passage for youngsters as they move into adolescence.[6] Many non-Western societies around the world have special ceremonies and customs that mark the passage from childhood to adulthood. Sometimes these are harmless, and in other cases they can be traumatic. Nevertheless they serve an important social function of growth and development: the official recognition of one's moving to a new phase of life. At present Americans have no general rite of passage for entering either adolescence or adulthood. Some might point to high school graduation, others to the age when a person can legally drive a car, still others to marriage or the legal drinking age as the rite of passage to adulthood. The fact is that we simply cannot agree when children move on to adolescence or even when adolescents become adults.

Thus Meier's recommendation is that we take the Jewish bar mitzvah and adapt it to the Christian community. If Jesus is our example, then this is biblical, given that his traveling to Jerusalem with his parents at age twelve probably involved a ceremony that was a predecessor to the bar mitzvah celebration. Meier cautions, however, that this not become an overly materialistic celebration, with presents and other party elements that often accompany modern bar mitzvahs.[7]

We attempted such a ceremony with one of our sons. Our pastor took a few minutes out of the evening service to interview our son and have him talk about his faith in front of the church. While we appreciated that attempt, perhaps it should have been a bit more elaborate. We suspect that one of these days there will be an entire book on how to conduct a Christian bar mitzvah, but for now we encourage you—if you have interest in such a ceremony—to read up on what various groups of Jews do for the occasion, and to use or adapt those aspects that fit well your faith. The main point of the ceremony is not just to celebrate adulthood, as it once was. (Our society, like most Western societies over the

6. In the book he and I wrote, titled *Raising Your Child.*

7. Meier speaks of a Jewish friend who was very disillusioned by such celebrations because they were little more than parties.

last hundred years or so, tells us that thirteen-year-olds are not adults, even though before our era most people would have assumed that teenagers were adults in most respects.) Rather, the main idea of such a ceremony is to underscore that the child has come of age and is now completely responsible in the area of faith and spirituality. This does not mean we stop encouraging church attendance or other spiritual activities, but it does mean that the child assumes a new level of responsibility for her own soul and spiritual health.

Moving from Conflict to Caring for Children and Parents

If a church is unhealthy, the conflicts in the church can produce the impression that church people are hypocritical. Even children can sense when God is not central to church life, and therefore they may come to believe that God is as irrelevant for daily life as he apparently is in church life. Those of us who are church leaders must actively resist the temptation to make the church an idol that replaces God. We must admit guilt in this area. Inconsistencies between what is said in church and how life is lived outside the church sow seeds of disgust and may help to bring about a rejection of faith.[8] We believe that taken as a whole, the Bible places first the personal relationship with God, second the family, and somewhere later on the priority list the organizational church.[9]

The person who regularly preaches is especially important in forming children's impressions of Christian faith. Preschoolers sometimes confuse the pastor with God, but this confusion is less likely as children get older. It is important for a pastor to spend time with the children in the church; the pastor's keeping a distance may result in children's seeing God as distant and unknowable. Forming this idea about God may not be a conscious decision by the child, but rather may be absorbed as an unconscious assumption that can stay with the child for years. As Catherine Stonehouse says, "At the deep core of their being the negative

8. Stonehouse, *Joining Children on the Spiritual Journey*, 67.

9. Jesus said the first great commandment is to love God with all your heart, soul, and strength; and the second commandment was to love the neighbor as self (Matt 19:19). Family members are perhaps the closest neighbors. The organizational church is not mentioned in the two commandments, or indeed in the entire ten, because it did not even exist at the time.

view of God will rule and their heart will not be able to grasp what their head knows."[10]

Research suggests that church attendance is gaining popularity. Children born since 1982 are less likely to be risk takers and more likely to join a church.[11] These are individuals likely to have small children and to desire high-quality ministry for their children. In the 1980s many churches missed the opportunity to reach out to baby boomers—the largest generation in American history—who were looking for churches that would minister effectively to their children. Now that the children of the boomers (who constitute a population "baby boomlet") are becoming parents, we must ask if the church is finally ready to take children seriously and to minister to their needs as well as to the needs of their parents. We believe it can if given sufficient encouragement in that direction.[12]

10. Stonehouse, *Joining Children on the Spiritual Journey*, 135.

11. Howe and Strauss, *Millennials Rising*.

12. While the recent history cited may be discouraging, I am encouraged by the recent upsurge of interest in children's spirituality, both in the books being sold and the number of research studies and conferences being held on the subject. While some of this interest represents a secular or New Age emphasis, there are also indications that some of the more forward-looking churches are becoming increasingly conscious of the needs of children. One such evidence is a national conference being held on Christian views of children's spirituality, for which I serve on the planning board. See the Web page at http://www.childspirituality.org/.

| TEN | # Walking and Talking
            # the Journey

Family Field Trips

FAMILIES TAKE VACATIONS, OR most of us do anyway. We hope your family is not an exception. There is much to be said for spending major chunks of time together, as often happens on vacations. Even if you and your kids do not spend every moment together during a vacation, it is likely you will spend several hours in the car, getting to your destination. Make that time count; don't let the kids listen to CDs or watch videos for the entire trip.

Vacation Bible School and Camps

While we spoke of church-centered activities in the previous chapter, we also need to examine church-related activities that are not routine services and classes. Many churches have summer Vacation Bible School (VBS), yet some parents do not take full advantage of this experience. You may want to follow carefully what is being taught during your church VBS to see how it may coincide with what you want your children to learn. During the VBS you can use some of the same topics in your teaching and activities at home with your kids. Usually several churches within a community will sponsor Vacation Bible School, and thus you may want to let your child have several such experiences. You may or may not want your child to experience the same curriculum twice at different churches. If she asks whether she can go to another church even if the curriculum is the same, it may be that repetition would be good or at least fun for her. On the other hand, the familiarity might make the VBS less than interesting. If you are considering the possibility of your child's going to two or more different Vacation Bible School programs, be sure they are all consistent with the theology and perspectives that you want your child to affirm. Talking with the pastor of an unfamiliar church, or with friends who attend, may help you determine whether a VBS program would be suitable. Do not assume that VBS will always be a positive experience for your child—the specific children who attend, as well as the theological bent of the church, teachers, and curriculum can make all the difference between a great experience and a negative one.

VBS can also be an opportunity for you to learn more about teaching children. Often those who create VBS curriculum know a good bit about how children learn, and you may get some good ideas by being involved as a teacher at your church for the week or so needed. Please be assured that there is no magic in teaching children. Sometimes parents convince themselves they cannot teach children, and sometimes parent-education programs may even make you feel less competent as a parent.[1] That is unfortunate, considering that the Bible generally assumes that parents are the best teachers (Prov 22:6). So sift what you learn about teaching if you volunteer to teach VBS or children's classes at church. Ask God to help you see what is true and what is not about teaching.

Camp meetings were once a powerful influence in American church life. The idea of taking a week to ten days off work; of traveling to a remote location where you camp in tents, trailers, and cabins; and of hearing messages by well-known speakers in the morning and evening and sometimes in the afternoon may seem rather archaic. While the camp meeting still exists in some areas, it is largely a thing of the past,[2] except in the recent variation called the music festival. Christian music festivals often draw thousands of people for several days of all-day music and preaching. They may fulfill some of the goals of the camp meeting—minus the times of quiet reflection and prayer between services.

Another variation of the camp meeting is the family camp, where families may attend a camp (sometimes a church-sponsored camp or a camp reserved by a church). The activities at family camp may be age specific, or they may include the whole family at one time. Family camps

1. Stonehouse, *Joining Children on the Spiritual Journey*, 38.

2. In *Mine Eyes Have Seen the Glory*, 4th ed., and his PBS television special by the same name. Randall Balmer visited several camp meetings that are still active. Though one particular camp is not mentioned in the book, the television special does include several scenes from the camp meeting I attended as a child in West Virginia, a camp founded by my grandfather in the 1920s. This particular excerpt of the film is available online, with the permission of the publisher, at: http://mountolivetcamp.ratcliffs.net/.

are usually held over a long weekend and generally provide recreational activities such as swimming, hiking, and competitive games. Time is often provided for family devotions or Bible studies, and resources for these activities may be included.

Another possible experience is the church camp or day camp for children. One study indicated that 87 percent of children who attend camps reported having a "rich and lasting experience," which doubled to tripled the rate for other Christian-education functions within the denomination studied.[3] One early study of children's camps indicated that character development was significant when specific goals were emphasized. Changes noted in the children included increased honesty, increased responsiveness to God as opposed to reliance upon parents, and increased Spirit-led morality as opposed to church- or rule-based behavior.[4]

Camping as a family without either the structure of a family camp or the separation of a church camp can also be a rich experience. Family camping without the structured "family camp" can be an invaluable experience; the natural world can teach important spiritual truths. Biblical characters often encountered God outdoors. Consider Moses in the wilderness learning discipline, patience, humility, and obedience to God. He later led the Israelites in the wilderness, so they learned to depend upon God completely. Later David wrote many psalms, no doubt inspired by the beauty around him, while tending sheep. John the Baptist lived in the desert, and people came this area of desolation to hear his insights received from God and to be baptized. Paul's experience in the Arabian area freed him from the constraints of day-to-day living so that he could receive a touch from the Lord that would prepare him for ministry. Even Christ ministered primarily outdoors and regularly sought the wilderness and solitary places in the wild to hear from his father.[5]

Camping helps the family listen to God by tuning out the interference of everyday life. The environment provides illustrations and object lessons that can yield insight into God and God's word. In the words of

3. Cited by Richard Troup and Joanne Brubaker, "Recreation and Camping for Children," 307–30. The denomination is not included in the citation, nor is the source.

4. This study, conducted in 1960, was conducted at a camp that included children, but it is not clear whether it was exclusively a children's camp, or if it involved families.

5. These examples are taken from a paraphrase by Cyd Quarterman of part of a book by Erik C. Madsen: *Youth Ministry and Wilderness Camping*.

Isaiah, all of creation sings God's praises (Isa 55:12). Activities that can help prompt such insights include horseback riding, biking, hiking, canoeing, rafting, kayaking, searching for rare plants or tracking animals, skiing or snowshoeing, following a creek, and taking pictures of nature. For starters, Cyd Quarterman lists nine object lessons, just as a beginning of the lessons that can be learned while camping:[6]

- Creeks and rivers: The forgiveness of God is ever flowing and cleans us.
- Flowers: Just as they reflect God's beauty, we need to reflect God's love (Matt 6:28), and the aroma of Christians should draw others to Christ.
- Grass: It reminds that our life on earth is temporary (Matt 6:30).
- Stars: May our light shine in the dark so that people will be drawn to our Lord.
- Birds: Their songs should remind us to praise God.
- Tree roots: Strength and nourishment come from rootedness in the Bible.
- Fruit trees: Bearing spiritual fruit is the result of a relationship with Christ.
- Sky: God's love is infinite and the sky is his canvas.
- Seeds: We are to plant faith seeds by sharing Christ with others.

Camps, music festivals, and camp meetings can be important experiences to share with your children. As with biblical holidays, they require a special time and place that is separate from the day-to-day routine. These special events are much like the biblical Feast of Tabernacles mentioned in chapter 9, when adults and children would assemble a makeshift structure of tree limbs and lumber, and live in them for a week or so.[7] The purpose was to recollect what God had done for their ancestors—for the people of Israel—as they camped in the wilderness

---

6. These are from personal correspondence with Cyd Quarterman, who teaches courses in the psychology department at Toccoa Falls College, Toccoa Falls, Georgia. I have added a few ideas to hers in the list.

7. In most cases there are brief visits to the "booth" rather than extended stays. In some cases children would camp out in these rough structures, and families might share an evening together in the small dwelling.

for forty years. As children, neither of us ever heard camp-meeting speakers make a connection between the biblical feast and the camp meeting, but it was there in the name of the main building: that building was called the tabernacle.

If you do take part in one of these special camp-meeting retreats, be available to your children if they have questions about something from a message, a song, or another experience. You might want to follow up each night on some key themes from the day as you get ready for bed in your trailer, tent, or cabin; although everyone may be too tired for this if it has been a long day. If nothing else, you might encourage discussion of what was learned as you make your way home from such a camp meeting.

One last location should be mentioned for camping: the backyard. Your ocean or postage stamp of green grass can be a wonderful place to camp. For some reason, children (at least before they are ten years old or so) often love to camp in the yard. Hanging a clothesline, draping it with a couple of blankets, and bringing sleeping bags into the makeshift tent can produce an imaginary safari into the wild for kids. As you settle in for the night, don't forget to tell your kids about the wild animals that could attack. (Okay, so dogs are probably the most vicious animals in most suburban areas.) But then do tell them about the protective care of Jesus when his disciples were in a small fishing boat on a large lake in the midst of a storm (Matt 8:23–27; Mark 4:35–40; Luke 8:22–25). Talk with them about their dreams and plans while emphasizing God's wonderful plans for them. Let the fun of camping in the "outback" be connected to the Christ of the raging sea.

A student who had several lively children told me of a place to camp that is even closer to home than the yard: the living room.[8] Every Friday night he made it a point to roll out the sleeping bags for his wife and five children and camp out all night with the kids. He pulled the plug on the television, and instead pulled out his guitar and they sang together for all they were worth. They took turns telling Bible stories and then family stories, and finally made up stories just for fun. They prayed together, ate snacks together, and slept together. They didn't need to fear beasts in the wild, just the family cat that might attack if they were too quiet. The kids looked forward to Friday night with Mom and Dad, at least until they

---

8. This idea comes from personal conversations with Jeff and Lisa Havlin, who regularly practiced this for a number of years.

became teenagers. Now that most of the kids are grown and have young-sters of their own, they probably have their own living room camps on Fridays as the tradition lives on. But we suspect they return home once in a while for a three-generation living room campout!

Music, Drama, and Television

Most churches have special times for music and at least one drama a year (the Christmas play and possibly an Easter play as well). The drama is likely to include children, and youngsters are still memorizing lines for those plays, just as we did when we were children in the 1950s and 1960s. These can be valuable experiences, as children act out roles of a persons or animals, sometimes even trees and shrubs.

The value of the experience is heightened when the drama imitates as closely as possible the original event. Unfortunately, churches do not often check out the historical details to be sure they have an ac-curate perspective on what occurred. For example, we must admit that we cringe a bit when churches use regular bread or homemade bread in depicting the Last Supper of Christ. Jewish people would never have used leavened bread at the Passover Seder, which is the context of the Last Supper. The Old Testament explicitly states that the bread was un-leavened, or what modern Jews call matzo. This is important because Jesus identified with the matzo; it has stripes, and "with his stripes we are healed" (Isa 53:5, KJV); it has holes just as Jesus was "pierced for our iniquities" (Isa 53:5, KJV); and finally it is without leaven just as Jesus was without sin (2 Cor 5:21). Now we are not legalists; we don't think God will punish the church that uses regular bread in communion or in drama (crackers would be closer to matzo than would normal bread), just as we do not think he would be angry if we substituted Kool-Aid for grape juice or wine. But the symbolism is not as clear, and substitutions reflect carelessness. It is possible that children may come away believing that communion is not all that important.

Use music and drama experiences to encourage your children to think about the spiritual themes emphasized. After such an experience, you might ask your children if they had a special spiritual experience during a music or drama event. If you felt especially close to the Lord during the special church event, talk to your children about that experi-ence and what it means to you.

To some extent you might try the same idea with television shows and music, although it is likely you may have some critique as well. Your kids are more likely to learn to be discriminating in their television viewing and CD listening if they hear you analyzing what you see and hear. Children are born imitators. During commercial breaks on television, talk with your children about what you heard and how it is consistent with or contradicts Scripture. Both principles and specific statements of Scripture can be used in the process. If you are watching a video or DVD, pause it occasionally and discuss what is happening, the moral elements involved, and how God might feel about what is portrayed or sung. This not only helps children become more discerning and thoughtful about what they watch, but also gives you an opportunity to clarify what they do not understand about the plot or the song. We know it is sometimes difficult to pause a movie or program for such discussion, but it can help children to understand things from a biblical perspective and can relieve confusion about what is being said or what is taking place. Movies, television shows, and music can be wonderful vehicles for learning, if parents make the effort and take the time to make it happen.

If you are watching a Christian show or even a nature program, it is possible that your child could have a spiritual experience at the time. We encourage you to let the child talk about it, if he or she so chooses, even if it means pausing the program or momentarily muting the sound. One must make decisions that count for eternity, and listening to your child relate a vivid experience with the Lord may be far more important than hearing the end of a show. We must confess we don't always think about such things from God's perspective; we often forget and shush the comments of my children during such programs. While most of the time the children's comments may not have eternal significance, we won't know if they are significant comments unless we listen to them carefully.

Farms and Fishing as Foundations of Faith Formation

Children better understand events in the Bible if they can relate them in some way to their own experiences. Some, perhaps even many, biblical accounts of events will make sense to rural children because there is some connection to the past. But for the child who grows up in the city and has few experiences in the country, some of the agriculture-based accounts in the Bible may be meaningless.

Yet even kids who grow up in more rural areas may not have the relevant experiences needed to understand the Bible. I (Don) grew up in a small town in a predominantly rural area, and many of my peers in school lived on farms. However, I did not get a strong taste of farm life until, during a family vacation, my family visited a distant relative who lived on a farm. The planting and harvesting, even milking the cows and feeding the animals were important experiences that even today help me better picture biblical events such as Jesus's parables of the different seeds (Matt 13:3–9) and of the weeds (Matt 13:24–30), the Bible verse that talks about a seed's dying before it can produce fruit (John 12:24), the connection of spiritual fruit with the farming process (1 Cor 3:4–7), and other descriptions in the Old and New Testaments.

As another example of our misunderstanding the settings of biblical stories, many of us have a misconception of the fishing that Jesus's disciples did. We suspect the majority of Christians have done more fishing with poles and hooks than with nets. In the movie *A River Runs Through It*, the main character comments (apparently with tongue in cheek) that he was sure his pastor father thought the disciples went fly-fishing. Yet in the accounts of Scripture, nets were more commonly used. If we want our children to vividly picture the gospel accounts, a visit to a boat with fishing nets (and ideally a trip out to sea as well) can help children picture the disciples and their fishing accurately. This can have important implications for understanding some of the metaphors Jesus used, such as the comparison of making disciples to fishing (Matt 4:19). Children who hear the story of Jesus's calling the first disciples sometimes assume Jesus was talking about rods, bait, and hooks, and this kind of thinking was even encouraged by well-meaning teachers in church who taught us to make the motions of casting with an imaginary pole while singing the song "I Will Make You Fishers of Men." But Jesus is certainly not suggesting that people have to be hooked by something to enter the kingdom of God, nor is he saying we must use bait to get people to accept Christ, and there is no implication that "fish" must be caught one by one. Instead, as he spoke with his fishermen disciples, he was speaking of casting nets out and bringing in many fish at once, minus the hooks and bait. Some of us, even as adults, have faulty pictures of what the Bible says because of inadequate past experiences. But a boat trip with fishermen that use nets (or even a video of such an experience) would give a more accurate background with which to understand biblical content precisely.

As you tell your children stories, and even in your own personal reading of the Scripture, we encourage you to think of the aspects of a situation described with which your children may be unfamiliar. Planning a vacation that includes one or more excursions that relate to biblical concepts can be a worthwhile effort, an effort that may pay off for a lifetime in the child's more accurate understanding of Scripture.[9]

Pilgrimages to the Holy Lands: Israel and Georgia

Children need connectedness. Family and home are usually the strongest connections for children, and faith may be more connected to these if most of the meaningful faith experiences occur at home with family. However, most of us—and quite possibly your children as well—also have a faith-centered connectedness to a church or another religious setting. Even though I (Don) described my struggle with a camp meeting in chapter 1 of this book, I must admit I also have a strong connectedness with that same camp. When I visit the grounds today, I remember some of the blessings of the camp: the good meals (I attribute my lifelong love of fresh tomato sandwiches to the camp), the fellowship while playing volleyball and baseball with other children, and the long talks late at night with a good friends. I recall the Nashville disk jockey who sold me an old guitar with a mouse hole in it at about age ten, I see a best friend cooking for the camp, and I even picture the first time I took Brenda to that camp. I see my grandfather, who founded the camp, rocking on the porch and perhaps thinking of his next sermon. I see my parents huddled with me and my brother in a little cabin that once housed an electric generator before public electricity became available. I remember choir practice for camp, as a distant relative of mine did her best to try to get local kids to have less of an Appalachian accent when they sang. And, yes, I remember many talks with God, including a good many at that old, dark altar rail in the tabernacle.

9. Of course there are some events in Scripture we may feel we understand accurately, and yet we do not, because we too readily assume the situation then was like our situation now. Sometimes study Bibles and Bible commentaries can open the window to the original context and thus correct misconceptions about the context of biblical events. There are also "manners-and-customs-in-the-Bible" books available at many Christian bookstores, and these can be helpful if they are not out of date. Beware! A number of books on this subject look new but are actually from the 1800s and may have a number of factual errors, unless they have been significantly updated.)

While my spiritual connection is perhaps strongest with that little campground, and I have taken my children to that camp and have tried to describe some of my feelings and memories, I realize they have no such connection with that place. These are long-ago recollections of a dad who is more than fifty years old: ancient history that means little to them.

But then there is Georgia. We lived there nineteen years; two of our three children were born there. Since we left, all of us have gone back to see the old friends, the house we built, much of it with our own hands as two little boys made their own backyard forts from the scrap lumber. (Our daughter would soon join the family after we had moved into the house.) The trips back to Georgia are not just to see familiar places and faces but to recall those events that have impacted our faith journey.

When we return to Georgia, we visit the churches we attended in that area. They are connected to our spiritual lives emotionally and perhaps even somehow in the spiritual realm. We can't say for sure, but it seems likely. During a recent summer we took our youngest back for the first time. It just seems part of being human. The word *pilgrimage* fits.

Memories are a reference point for the present and the future. They provide meaning and guidance. Even bad memories help guide us to avoid such things in the future. The meaning of remembering an experience comes from realizing what we experienced as bad really was pretty bad, and what was good really was good. The connectedness comes from both the good and the bad as they point us to events or feelings about which we should say, "Yes, that's me," and other memories we leave behind. Affirm and forgive; that's the stuff of which connections are made. We see it more clearly with the passing of time, and when we return we see the past through new eyes—eyes that are wiser for the new places and the different experiences since leaving the past behind.

While my (Don's) wistful recollections about West Virginia are adult reflections of my childhood, for our children it is Georgia that brings the spiritual and other memories. It is good for them to revisit their past from time to time, just as it is for me to do so. If your family has moved in the last few years, go back. Go back and take your children. Let them remember and reexperience the joys and pain from their past, and they will better understand your tears and smiles when you return to your childhood places of the Spirit. They will begin to understand, if only a little now, and perhaps a lot better later.

How you deal with your past will influence your children. Grudge bearing is an inherited trait—our kids will inherit it by imitating the example they see in us. But then forgiveness and joy can also be inherited traits; they too can be copied. Go back to your childhood homes and to the homes your children remember. Go back to your children's grandma and grandpa, to the pastors and the people in the churches of the past. Love them; forgive them; remember them. Perhaps your children will someday do the same. If you are fortunate, it will happen before you leave this life.

Now for a very different pilgrimage. When I (Brenda) visited Israel, I wrote in my journal:[10]

> When I was praying at the Wailing Wall I was so impressed with the women around me. Many were orthodox and were going through their prayer books while bowing at the wall. Some refused to turn their back on the wall, instead they backed away from it while continuing to bow. Obviously they were showing great respect and reverence for this holy place and were quite devout but their absence of joy in the midst of their religious observance grieved my heart. One woman at the Wall was the self-appointed religious policewoman (maybe a modern day feminine Pharisee). She kept a scowling watch on everyone and would scold one for showing too much flesh, while chastising another for not behaving appropriately. Other women were tending children while praying. I saw tears, piety, faith, and religious duty but no joy. I was overwhelmed with concern for them and prayed that they soon would see Him.

This is not West Virginia or Georgia; it is obviously a very different place, a place with which most of us are not familiar. Here the connection with God and with the past is not from personal experiences in Israel, but rather from the Bible, and from our understanding of the God of the Bible, and from Christ, who walked there, and who is personally involved in our lives. Furthermore, there is another connection: God's chosen people, whose lives we see portrayed in Scripture, whose words we read in Scripture. Just as the Bible describes, many of them are very religious, yet how much they need a Savior!

Children need to see the emptiness of a life without Christ. If we shield our kids from those of other faiths and those who are unbelievers,

10. The full text of the journal is located at this Web site: http://www.brenda.ratcliffs.net/stonesbones.pdf.

they may falsely assume that much of the rest of the world is like us. We need to help them see not only that the world not like us, but that false and misleading prejudices are everywhere. Those were the prejudices Jesus spoke against most often. Again I quote from my journal:

> While visiting Shepherd's Field just outside of Bethlehem, I was impressed by a young Arab girl, carrying a goat. It is hard for those of us so influenced by the Western media to understand that not every Arab in Israel is a Palestinian or even subscribes to Palestinian politics. In fact, I met one Arab businessman who is so disillusioned with the Palestinian Authority that he is considering a move to America! There are many innocent people, including the children, who are caught in the middle of the age-old struggle between the sons of Isaac and the sons of Ishmael. They are desperate for peace.

Children, at least when they are small, know little more than what we let them see and experience. We need to shield our children from the worst of the evil in the world, but perhaps we need to let them see some of the results of evil in the world. Children need to see that there are Arabs who are good as well as those who are not so good, and that some of God's people are good while others that are less than the best. (You can take this to refer to Israel or to your local church, whichever you prefer, as it is true for both).

We can talk about the evils of prejudice to our children, but they may not appreciate how bad that evil really is until they see it when an Asian girl in class is teased because of her accent or appearance. We can describe the millions of hungry children around the world, but it may not impact our children significantly until they see for themselves. Our kids need to see the families and children that live in a dump just across the border from the beautiful state of California. They need to see the impoverished youngsters in the inner city, and the homeless children with or without parents. They need to see it on video, but they also need to be there to smell the awful smells, to see the ragged clothes, to touch the dirt that is everywhere, to see what could have been their lives if not for the grace of God.

And then they need to do something about it. They need to join a mission group to help build homes for the needy in Haiti. They need to read the letters from the Compassion child, and write their own letters in response. They need to pray for the friendships that came from the visit to Haiti and the World Vision child we support. They need to lend a hand at the soup kitchen for the homeless and poor. They need to sing and share a testimony at the nursing home. They need to give their nickels and dimes in the offering for missionaries. But they probably won't do it unless they do it with us. Indeed we probably would not want them to do it unless we are there by they side.[11] And that is the way it should be. They will pray, they will give, and they will go if we pray, we give, and we go as well.

11. Again, recall the conclusions of Roehlkepartain in *The Teaching Church*: children are more likely to affirm parental faith if they are involved with the family in social-service projects.

ELEVEN

Potential Faith Partners

Siblings, Grandparents, and Friends

M ANY PEOPLE CAN HAVE a powerful influence upon the spiritual development of your children. Sometimes the influence is positive, at other times it can be negative. To some degree anyone who knows your child can and will influence her, one way or the other. Even when they ignore God—perhaps especially when they ignore God—the message is conveyed that He is unimportant, irrelevant to the situation. The assumption that God is uninvolved and easily ignored may be more detrimental than outright rejection of God. Rejection at least implies that something or Someone worth talking about is rejected; ignoring something or Someone implies that it/He may not even be worth talking about.

Siblings: Rivalry . . . and Revelry

Brothers and sisters can be blessings or curses. Usually they are something in between, or a combination of both. At certain ages a brother or sister can help in spiritual development, such as when they share their own mistakes and struggles. They may be transparent enough to talk about unfortunate outcomes of wrong and sinful decisions. They can also point out the positive consequences of right thinking and behavior. These moments of sharing represent family life at its best. We wish they occurred more often.

Too often siblings work against your efforts to encourage spiritual growth and development. Kids can even team up against your best efforts at spiritual nurture, such as when they lobby for questionable movies. Older brothers and sisters may want to take on your role of parent, and that can multiply the number of bosses the younger child perceives.

Sibling bosses may not encourage biblical and godly attitudes, values, and behavior. In contrast, older children can align with the younger child against you and against what is best for their spiritual health. Perhaps the worst-case scenario happens when a child aligns with the other parent against you and what is best for that child. Child-child coalitions can be unpleasant and difficult, but parent-child coalitions against the other parent can be very demoralizing and defeating spiritually unless of course the parent-child coalition forms to protect itself against abuse by the other parent.

We're afraid there are no magic solutions to eliminate spiritually counterproductive sibling or parental influences on children. Prayer, and lots of it, is needed. Being honest about your feelings can help, although it is important not to demean any of the children in expressing frustration. I (Don) had a childhood friend whose mother, a Christian I believe, struggled continually with her children, partly because their father was not a Christian, and partly because her children formed a strong coalition and put her down regularly. I don't know what discipline she used, but I do recall her screaming, "I wish you had never been born" to her son, my friend, on several occasions. I don't want to be too critical of her, because she was bearing a burden I have never borne, but I know such statements—made in exasperation—must have hurt my friend deeply, although he never showed it. He covered the hurt, at least the hurt from hearing that statement the first time when he was a child, by calling her an obscene name to her face. If she had tried to discipline, I'm sure her husband or an older sibling would have physically hurt her. I think she wanted to have a Christlike attitude, but it was incredibly difficult for her. Eventually there was a divorce, but the old patterns persisted. I don't know if there was a psychological solution. I certainly didn't know all the family dynamics, but situations arise in which there seem to be no answer apart from "muddling through."

God wants brothers and sisters to encourage one another spiritually by precept and example. Perhaps this is a message that needs to be communicated early to children. We all know that "no man is an island," and children need to see their spiritual responsibility and spiritual role in relation to their brothers and sisters (and that does not mean becoming a rule-enforcer). Scripture speaks of spurring one another on to love and good works as the reason for "assembling yourselves together" (Heb 10:24–25). We believe that this teaching applies to a household as much as to a church, because the earliest churches were households, with the possible additions of neighbors and visitors. Perhaps parents need to use this passage to teach about the kinds of relationships God desires between brothers and sisters. Other passages that teach what God desires in all human relationships (such as Rom 12:18) can also be helpful.[1]

Children are more likely to work with you if they see good reason to do so. Thus positive results may be motivating. We don't mean that you necessarily give a candy bar to a child for cooperating, but you may want to give some thought to privileges for a child who takes responsibility in a productive manner. This is a very biblical concept. Jesus expressed the idea of differing levels of responsibility at the end of the parable of the talents (Matt 25:14–28, also see Luke 12:48). Older siblings need to be informed not only of their responsibility to encourage younger brothers and sisters, but also that their lives and relationships are more a testimony than is anything they might say.

Sometimes we as parents need to be a bit tolerant of sibling differences. I (Don) grew up in a family where, for most of my childhood, I was essentially an only child. Thus I found myself less prepared for dealing with relationships between my three children. On the other hand, Brenda grew up in a family of four children, and for a while they also had a fifth "sibling" who stayed with them. As the oldest child in the family, she had plenty of experience with sibling rivalry and a strong understanding of when a parent should settle the rivalry, or when a parent needs to back off and let the children work things out for themselves. Thus I had much to learn in this area. We have sometimes used Bible stories and passages of Scripture to help our children settle their differences. In the process of learning from these texts, they found that the Bible is extremely relevant for the most intimate relationships: with parents, siblings, and one's own children.

Brenda and our children also taught me about revelry. At times when a good tickle fight or pillow fight can relieve tension or just be plain old fun. Of course these can get out of hand, and parents may need to intervene. It is especially embarrassing when we must end what we helped begin! Healthy families can wrestle and play with one another but

1. Use Scripture with care, of course, that you do not distort the original meaning. Especially look at the context—what comes before and after a given verse—to be more certain you are understanding correctly. It may be tempting to use the verse Galatians 5:15 with a child who bites, but I don't presume that is what Paul is talking about! (Even if he were, the idea of devouring the sibling may be appealing to some kids!)

also know when to stop, hopefully before the tears begin. If things get extreme but not hurtful, stories from family times can become legends. In our family, the piece of cake stuck to the ceiling after a wild contest of the wills . . . Well, it quite literally "takes the cake"!

Is God in the revelry? The Bible clearly portrays situations where revelry is wrong (such as the golden calf incident in Exodus 32) but also times when exuberance is godly, such as during the wedding feast Jesus attended (John 2:1–11). The contrast between these incidents comes in the intention behind the revelry: the first involves worship of a forbidden idol, the second an exuberant time of laughing and merriment. (See the movie *Fiddler on the Roof* for more examples of godly merriment.) When children are having an uproariously good time, and the focus is on the enjoyment of one another, this may be considered a time of fellowship. When a parent gets involved, the message for the others involved is clearly, "This is okay; this is right." Parents can show an approval much like God's approval. As we mentioned earlier, our earliest concepts of God take on qualities of one or both parents (see chapter 4). By our involvement in the revelry, we may be communicating—unconsciously rather than overtly—that God affirms family fun. It is an important responsibility for us as parents to be careful to communicate such affirmation when things are indeed good from a biblical perspective, and to intervene and stop what is happening when it is not for the best. Children are learning about the two contrasting aspects of God in the process of our interventions: they see on the one hand the justice of God, and on the other hand the love and mercy of God. Children need to experience both of these, for one without the other gives a distorted view of the Almighty. Participating in godly revelry with our kids can help us communicate the possibility of God's intense involvement in our lives, and his lively love. The exuberance of lively worship is not very different from the exciting revelry of hide and seek. One might even see parallels between what Francis Thompson (1859–1907) describes as the "Hound of Heaven" and chasing your youngster around the house, completed by "I gotcha."

Child Culture

The chase games of childhood are similar to what some have called "the culture of childhood," or sometimes "peer culture."[2] Child culture em-

2. This was one of the main topics of my dissertation and is reflected in some of my

phasizes play, the accepted ways of acting with friends and others of the same age, and an open flexibility that permits a wide variety of behavior, some of it probably unacceptable to parents and other adults. Child culture is seen in pretend punching and fighting between boys, as well as in jump-rope rhymes and other girl-centered games. Child culture during middle childhood encourages boys to play with boys, and girls with girls. It can involve poking fun at others, as well as some children's dominating others. It is tribal, emotional, playful, sensuous, and frivolous. Some believe it is an elaboration of the play in early childhood.

Children teach children this child culture; rarely would a parent or teacher be found teaching such things. Siblings often teach it, but probably more often it is similar-age peers who instill and encourage child culture. This culture is usually opposed to the culture of school, which requires children to follow classroom routine, submit to adults, and accept the values of adult society. School culture is more institutional, rational, serious, mechanical, and task-centered than child culture. Whereas one sees child culture very clearly on an elementary-school playground, one observes school culture in most classrooms.

At home the child may sometimes experience something closer to child culture, and at other times something more like school culture. When we speak of teaching our children, we can be tempted to think of our teaching as fitting the school-culture model. While we don't rule out some formal teaching, we suggest that that the spiritual training of and the influence over children can also be like some aspects of child culture, and that sometimes our parental teaching will not be either clearly school culture or child culture. We have even wondered if there is something that might be called a "home culture" that is different from either child or school culture.

When you teach your child about your beliefs and talk with one another about spiritual experiences and how faith relates to life, are you more like a teacher in a classroom or like a friend? While parents have a distinctive role in loving and encouraging their children as well as in using discipline and example to shape behavior, it is possible that when discussing and experiencing faith-related issues you will be more like a teacher or more like a peer. If you choose the teacher role, you will probably emphasize thinking and understanding more than experience.

writings about children in church as well as in school; see Ratcliff, "Peer Culture and School Culture Theory," 57–76.

There will be greater seriousness about the task, and you and your child will see accomplishing the task as its goal. But there may be tension and possible frustration in the process. It is important to note that this is the result of the teaching role, not of the topics considered. We believe that if your youngster sees spirituality as a task to accomplish, then it is more likely to be done like schoolwork: in periods of concentrating on the task, then moving from that world into the real world disconnected from spiritual matters. You may find she talks with you about things you and she believe, rather than discussing the daily walk with God or spiritual experiences. Again, the tone of such conversations has to do with the teacher role that has been chosen, not with the quality of faith that is involved.

By contrast, if you choose to interact with your children in the role of peer, you will find less emphasis upon beliefs and ideas about God, church, the Bible, prayer, and so on. Instead discussion will be experience oriented, and emotional aspects of faith are likely to emerge. Discussions will be less task oriented. There may be a playfulness about your discussions and interactions, and this can have a place in parent-child interaction. Even talking about a Bible story, acting it out, or dancing to a related song with your child can produce fun and laughter for both of you. The positive emotions that accompany the experience are likely to transfer to the child's ideas about God and about living the Christian life. But this quality of interaction in regard to faith raises the danger of spirituality's becoming frivolous to the child, who may learn to minimize its importance.

Strengths and weaknesses exist in both parental roles (teacher or friend). Ideally you can combine these roles into a distinctive parental role, but at any given moment you may be more like a teacher or more like a peer. Your children may become playful and silly when you want them to be serious. Or you may be in a more playful mood when your child wants information or a serious discussion. We have found that when such mismatched moods occur, it often helps to step outside the role you desire and explain the difference between you and the child at that moment.

For example, we could have said to one of our sons when he was very young, "Son, I know you want to play and have fun, but it is bedtime, and we have just a few minutes for a story and prayer." However, by giving this example, we don't want to leave the impression that you should always ask the child to change roles. Before deciding which role to take, silently ask God to guide you to the appropriate parental role, and consider what is best for your child at the moment as well as the impact that the moment may have on the future and on your relationship. While my son is teasing and having fun, it may be that our planned serious activities can be placed on hold for a few minutes. After some silliness and laughter together, he will connect with us better and be more receptive to what we want him to learn. Some laughter, followed by milk and cookies, may result in the child's greater willingness to be reflective and, for example, to talk about struggles with his friends and school.

An important implication of this topic of parental roles and child responsiveness is that the role taken may influence what kind of learning and other activity will take place. While one can learn through fun and games as well as through serious instruction, each parental role will facilitate a specific kind of learning. If levity is the only association with God, the spiritual life may never become serious and reflective. At worst, God can become a joke. On the other hand, if all discussion and activity related to faith is serious, the child may come to conclude that God doesn't like fun and joy. An always-somber, uninteresting faith can be easy to reject. What is learned may be communicated as much or more at the emotional level than at the mental level. In other words, your children may feel that topics or times related to God must be serious, even if they think and talk about spiritual things as being sometimes fun and at other times more solemn. If you want your child to understand and relate to God in his fullness and with the breadth of human emotions (a wide spectrum of emotions is reflected in the Psalms, for example), the child needs to experience faith-related activities with you at both ends of the spectrum (lively as well as quiet activities), and at many points in between these extremes.

A very important aspect of any decision about your role has to do with your reading your child's cues accurately. Sometimes you or your child can miss the cues from each other about which role is in place, and the mismatch can produce frustration for both of you. Eye contact, tone of voice, facial expression, posture, physical distance, gesture—all these can signal the mood and role expectation of your child. Good parents hear with their eyes as well as their ears. Of course you may use these senses in combination with your words and touch to help the child shift from one role to the other. The child needs to read the cues you offer, and you may need to explain how you are showing which role you are taking and thus the role the child should accept. But it is equally important—perhaps most important—for you to read the child's cues, as well as for you to ask God for guidance about whether you or the child should shift roles. You want your child to know that you are approachable, be approachable even at inconvenient times, and ensuring your approachability is likely to require you to shift roles. On the other hand, the child's desire that you shift roles may not be as urgent as she thinks. Accurately reading such interpersonal cues is an important aspect of any relationship, and is very important when it comes to teaching faith and sharing spiritual concerns with your children.

Thus positive spiritual parenting may involve a more teacher-like role at certain times more of a friend-like role at other times, and a distinctive parental role at still other times. An example of a distinctive parent role is kissing your child goodnight. We suspect that neither her teacher nor her friends would do this. Actually it is possible that teachers and peers would rarely if ever even talk to the child about personal faith and spiritual experience, and thus such talks would be part of the parental role. One aspect of the parent role can be to raise special topics and conversations, but another is the ability to shift from the teacher to the friend role, or shift from the friend to the teacher role, when the child needs you to change. But perhaps most important of all, the parent role fundamentally involves love. Disciplining, teaching, friendship, being an example—all these have their place. But of all virtues that parents exercise with their children and try to instill in their children, "the greatest of these is love" (1 Cor 13:13).

Grandparents and Substitutes

An old quip that says that the reason grandparents and their grandchildren get along so well is because they have a common enemy. Hopefully that isn't the case in your family! Your parents can be very important in the spiritual development of your child. Those who have analyzed generational influences (such as describing baby boomers in contrast to Generation X or Generation Y) suggest that generations repeat themselves every fourth generation. In other words, there are similarities between you and your great-grandparents in relation to key values, ideas, and even experiences. If this is the case, then grandparents and their grandchildren may find one another interesting because the children of your children will resemble the characteristics of the grandparents of your children. We are not sure we completely agree with this theory, but it is an interesting idea and perhaps there is something to it.[3]

Grandparents have the potential for confirming the faith that you try to share with your child and for elaborating that faith. Godly grandparents can encourage the spiritual development of children by describing their own experiences before and after salvation, including key moments of spiritual growth. This can create an expectancy in your children that God may work in their lives at crucial turning points as well.

Grandparents can tell stories of the parents' early lives and struggles. As a result, your children may more readily connect with you as they come to understand that you were once children as they are, and encountered some of the same issues they experience. In the teen years your children may believe that their own experience is completely unique, but until that time kids are likely to see some similarities.

Grandparents can help supply family identity, as they speak of their own parents and other relatives. The good and the bad are scrutinized in the family legacy of stories. This backdrop for the family enriches a sense of continuity, that children are connected both to the past and to the future generations.

I (Don) remember so clearly my grandparents on the Ratcliff side of the family. When I was small, they would tell stories about faraway places and distant times that filled my head with wonder. The stories of relatives good and evil impressed me, even though sometimes the stories seemed larger than life, at least larger than my limited life. The stories accentuated the difference between the desirable and the repugnant by detailed accounts of the lives of relatives. In other words, they taught me morality.

If they are Christians, grandparents can supply a different perspective on faith, a faith that is the same faith but formed in a different time and perhaps in different places. This can open the door to your children's moving beyond just accepting your faith to realizing Christian belief and practice fit every generation a bit differently. This may be a concept that they will later draw upon in adolescence when, hopefully, they have a faith distinctly theirs, a walk with God that may vary from yours and your parents' yet be an authentic expression of a relationship with God.

3. Howe and Strauss, *Generations*.

It is also important to note that more grandparents than ever before are rearing their grandchildren.[4] Sometimes this is a shared task with one of the parents, but many are now doing it alone. There can be many reasons for this, from an undesired pregnancy to less than fully responsible parents. This once was more of an ethnic phenomenon; but these days, people of all ethnic backgrounds are childrearing—again. Having older parents can result in children's being more conservative. It can be less exciting for children when the grandparents tire quickly. Overall, however, there do not seem to be many—if any—negative consequences for the children. Giving up the freedom of the "empty nest" may be disappointing for some grandparents, but for others parenting during late middle age and the "golden years" is more fulfilling than retirement. Difficult lessons learned from the first set of kids can make grandparents much better the next time around.

What about grandparents who are less than ideal? What if they undermine the Christian values you work so hard to instill? Separation may be best in this case. When occasional contact is required, explain to your children the need to pray for their grandparents and not to follow their example. Sometimes children can influence grandparents when no one else can, but the influence may also go in the opposite direction (from the grandparents to the grandchildren). What is crucial is to realize that while you should honor your parents (Exod 20:12), the Scripture says that children should obey their parents (generally in the Bible the child officially became adult much earlier than today; by age twelve or thirteen youngsters were of marriageable age). You are under no obligation to obey misguided directives from your parents; God's perspective is very clear on this (see Luke 14:26 and 18:29). While the sins of the grandparents can influence their grandchildren and even great-grandchildren (Exod 20:5), it is also clear that we can stand against that influence and our efforts to cancel those influences can be passed on generation after generation as well (Exod 20:6).

If your parents live at a distance, it may be that they will only be able to visit once in a while. Telephone and e-mail conversations between grandparents and grandchildren may help keep the connection alive, and at key times your parents may be able to provide long-distance encouragement for your kids, especially in times of crisis. Sometimes substitute grandparents may be available at church or by visiting a nearby

4. HDEV, 306.

nursing home. Your adopting some "second parents" at church may help encourage "grandparenting" by godly senior citizens who will encourage spiritual growth in your children. Your children may even reach out to the "grandparents" and other elderly people who need comfort, help, and encouragement. As mentioned earlier, this may open the door to family projects that express the Christian faith in the form of tangible assistance.

The Spiritual Influence of Friends

We spoke earlier of the influence that child culture has on many children. Often that influence comes through friends who teach the rhythms of rough-and-tumble play ("play fighting"), jump-rope rhymes, and the other games that go with child culture. One major difficulty here may be that child culture often involves sexualized themes, sometimes songs and rhymes that either can be taken two ways or are even quite explicit.

I (Don) once had a couple eleven-year-old girls visit my college class to demonstrate some of the current rhymes used in such activities. They went through the first two verses as they twirled an imaginary jump rope. When they came to the third verse, they stopped briefly, blushed a bit, and said, "We better not do that verse." Of course the verse had some off-color content, and they felt it was a bit too much for my college students! (I suspect many of my college students already knew the lines.)

While the lyrics, dances, and rhymes of child culture sometimes are undesirable, child culture appears to be fading in recent years. Girls do not jump rope as much as they once did. Boys are also somewhat less likely to engage in rough-and-tumble play and other informal games. Children do not go out and play as much, and thus you see less spontaneous dancing, acting, and other aspects of child culture. As a result, more and more children are overweight (although eating habits probably contribute to this as well). To compound the problem, many schools have decreased or eliminated recess, while there is increased use of computers, television and videos, video games, and other activities that are not very active. Encourage your children to be more active by limiting their access to computers and television, but make sure they don't go down the street to a friend's house and use their computer or television. Monitor what they do and what they learn as they are with other children. Better yet, go out and play with them regularly; it's a good way to connect with them emotionally and may pave the way for real-life applications of biblical principles in their activities. Perhaps we need some Christian jump-rope rhymes!

Friends can be helpful or detrimental spiritually. Peer pressure begins by the early elementary years, perhaps even earlier, and peaks at about age eleven or twelve. Interestingly, one research study indicates that children see their peers as less religious than they see themselves, and thus the expectations of the group tend to pull all or most of the children away from spiritual vitality.[5] Children too often make fun of faith, tear down one another with name- calling, and participate in bullying.[6] While parents may not be able to completely eliminate such detrimental influences, we can at least try to minimize them. Overall, however, the research emphasizes a positive relationship between friendship and spirituality.[7]

We think it is important to monitor activities carefully to be sure they are healthy not only spiritually but also emotionally and physically. We have talked with parents of children who attended a youth group at church in which a full-time youth pastor regularly pointed them out as key sinners in the group. This brought gales of laughter from other kids. The young people continued to attend and didn't tell parents because of fear that their friends would reject them. They suffered emotionally, yet the senior pastor refused to intervene directly until the church board got involved, and even then no apology was made to the children who were hurt, and no correction or explanation was given to the other children who attended. We have also heard, again from those directly involved, about "Bible studies" that turned out to be sessions tearing down parents' values or even teaching witchcraft. Be careful of the friends your children keep, even if they are in the church! Yet research evidence also shows that increased spiritual and religious interest among children can be associated with friendships in a local church.[8]

While you may not have as much influence on your children's choice of friends when they get into junior high, high school, and college, you can influence the friends your youngsters have earlier in life. Screen them carefully. While finding children with competent, discern-

5. Hyde, *Religion in Childhood and Adolescence*, 238.

6. See Cram, *Bullying*.

7. Schwartz, et al. "Mentors, Friends, and Gurus," 310–23.

8. Hyde, *Religion in Childhood and Adolescence*, 239.

ing parents is important, there are fine people who do not know how to parent, and there are individuals who look great from the outside but are thoroughly compromised in their home life. Parents who are very conservative may not automatically have safer children or homes; indeed some children from such homes may rebel and become some of the worst influences. Child abuse, including sexual abuse, occurs more often that we might think among very conservative religious people, and often these children will introduce their friends to the evil.

We are not suggesting that you become paranoid and fearful of all other families and their children. But be careful. Occasionally monitor the conversations and play of your children with their friends by listening to or watching their activities from time to time, perhaps from a location that does not reveal you are there. Spot-checking occasionally can relieve fears of possible problems. Perhaps you can invite children to your house who you know are spiritually sensitive and have good moral character.

This is not to imply that unchurched children are to be avoided. Situations may arise where your children can be a positive influence on such youngsters. But my experience is that if you put two kids together, one good and one not so great, any friendship that develops tends to move the good child towards the one who is not so wonderful. On the other hand, if you have time and interest, you might consider having neighborhood clubs where children are introduced to the gospel message and encouraged to grow spiritually. If an older child (even a teenager) is more mature spiritually, he or she may be able to teach younger children. Intergenerational friendships among youngsters several years apart can be spiritually productive for both the older and younger child.[9] In addition, you may have a powerful influence on neighborhood children, and perhaps your child will as well. But to the extent possible, encourage the closest friendships between your youngster and spiritually and emotionally healthy peers.

In chapter 2 we spoke of the "numinous": the sense of the holy, the otherworldly, of mystery, awe, satisfaction, and fascination—or the spiritual experience common to all humans. A sense of the numinous, a spiritual experience if you will, can accompany experiences that friends may have. It can come from the thrill of doing something daring, tak-

9. Stonehouse, *Joining Children on the Spiritual Journey*, 89.

ing chances when there is no good reason for doing so.[10] The fun with friends may have spiritual overtones in the form of the numinous. Among Christian friends, the numinous may involve the Holy Spirit's work in the form of close fellowship and the developing of a deep love between friends. Or the numinous can just be overwhelming excitement from, say, taking a carnival ride with a friend. The numinous can also be the Enemy at work, in the form of friendships that influence children towards the use of illegal drugs, toward bullying others, toward rebellion against authority, or toward making fun of people who are not their friends.

God wants our children and us to live in the numinous of the Holy Spirit, to share that experience of the numinous with others who hold our faith, and to approach non-Christians in sharing our faith with others. The numinous may not be something we can control, but it can cement a friendship. If the friendship is one that God desires, then the numinous can make our children better for it; if the friendship is contrary to God, the numinous may be the work of the Enemy and may limit or even destroy what God wants to do.

Friends can be a powerful influence for good or evil. Friendships made during the childhood years often last into junior high and high school. Monitor friendships carefully, and be cautious about the friendships that are permitted. Check out both the friend and the family, and pray that God will show you which friendships your children should cultivate and which friendships need to be discouraged.

Spiritual Development and Schools

Most parents have three general options in relation to school choice, although a few have a couple more. You can send your children to the local public school, which is by far the most common choice among American Christians today. A second alternative is to send your kids to a Christian school. This is less an option for some Christian parents because of the costs as well as the limited availability of Christian schools in some areas. It may require a considerable commute to take your children to a high-quality school. A third alternative is homeschooling, which increased in

10. This is an aspect of adolescence often overlooked by researchers but present in hopefully less extreme forms during childhood and adulthood. See Lightfoot, *The Culture of Adolescent Risk-Taking*.

popularity dramatically during the 1980s and 1990s and continues to be a viable option for a small segment of Christian parents. A fourth possibility, rarely considered in the United States, is to send your children to a boarding school. This is most likely to be given consideration by missionaries, although an increasing number of missionaries are now turning to homeschooling or correspondence courses.[11]

Your child's spiritual development is likely to be affected by your school choice. But how much spiritual influence do schools have on children? Are children who attend Christian schools or home schools more likely to grow spiritually than children who attend public schools? You can argue it both ways. You could say that those who attend Christian schools have a Christian environment, with a Christian teacher and with peers who are probably Christians. The kids usually have at least one Bible class and chapel, which should encourage better understanding of the Scriptures and a stronger walk with God. There is also the potential for Scripture and Christian views to be infused in all subjects studied, not just in the Bible class or in chapel. These same arguments can be made for homeschooling, only the case is stronger because you control the curriculum as well as the peer contacts. This sounds like Christian schools and home schools should win the debate, hands down.

But let's see if we can make the opposite case. The child who attends public school should be more likely to develop spiritually because he or she confronts the real world, and thus faith is tested; and if it passes, it will be stronger because of these challenges. Furthermore, Scripture tell us that we are to be in the world but not of it; that is, we are to provide a witness to unbelievers. How can a child do that if everyone she is with throughout the day is a Christian? Public schools need Christians to be "salt and light" to the world, and some public schools have a number of Christian teachers, and even administrators who are Christians. Of all the teachers I (Don) had from kindergarten through twelfth grade, only one I suspect may not have been a Christian. In the area where I now live, many Christians work in the public schools because my university produces so many public-school teachers who end up staying in this general area.

So you can make the case for all three options: Christian education, homeschooling, or public education. A key factor that needs to be considered is the research of the spiritual impact of Christian schools. It

---

11. This is in part due to charges of abuse at some boarding schools, as noted earlier.

makes sense that children should be powerfully influenced in a positive direction by Christian schools, but is this what generally happens? A clear-cut general answer arises to this question, although "the devil is in the details." We have to hedge a bit in terms of specific situations and certain aspects of spiritual development.

A major summary of nearly two hundred research studies covering children in many countries and at many Christian schools representing many denominations provides surprisingly consistent results. The summary concludes that religious schools have little or no influence on a child's spirituality and faith, although some positive influence does occur when the child comes from a strong Christian home.[12] The home life is much more influential upon a child than the Christian school. In other words, if a child attends a Christian school (under the assumption that the school is of fairly high quality and that the child comes from a Christian home with a strong emphasis on encouraging the child's faith), the school is likely to have some positive influence on the child. However, some of the research suggests that he or she needs to attend the school for several years in order to come under a positive influence, and then that influence is most likely to be small compared with the influence of the home.

Parents who send their children to a Christian school and do little or nothing at home related to the child's faith and spiritual growth are unlikely to receive much if any benefit from the children's attending a Christian school. Most non-Christians who attend Christian schools do not become Christians and are likely to have a negative influence on the Christian children that attend the school. When a school environment exerts a positive influence on the child, that influence is more likely to be the result of the general climate of the school (supportive, encouraging) rather than of classes in religion or chapel.

Of course, one must also allow for exceptions to this rule; there are children who come from non-Christian homes, who do become Christians and perhaps even influence their parents toward the Christian faith as a result of attending a Christian school. Some children are very positively influenced by Christian school even if parents do little or nothing of a spiritual nature at home. And for some children, the influence is more immediate. But these exceptions are apparently not the most com-

12. Hyde, *Religion in Childhood and Adolescence*, 293–335 (chapter 14: "The Religious Influence of Schools").

mon result. In most cases it is the family rather than the Christian school that will influence the child most in terms of spirituality development.

However, we need to hedge a bit on these conclusions, as the author of the summary article also did.[13] Some of the research studies were weakly designed. In some cases the researchers included schools where teachers disliked religion classes so that teachers with the least experience and lowest status might teach such a class. This could produce results that suggested less influence than what the school might have if the best teachers taught those religion classes. Another common flaw in the research is that schools can be very different from one another. We personally know of a so-called Christian school that was a dumping ground for kids expelled from public schools; it had more drug and sex problems than the public schools did, for obvious reasons! We have also seen Christian schools that are harsh and oppressive. One of the schools to which we sent our children made compromises that were spiritually and emotionally detrimental, and we ended up withdrawing two of our children and sending them to public schools that proved to be more healthy for them.

There are fine Christian schools that are neither harsh nor indulgent, and that require all students to be Christians. These schools can have a strong influence upon children for the good, especially if the personalities of the child and teacher are a good mix, if the other children are accepting of your child and a positive influence, and if your family resources are not drained completely.

The best research summary to examine what makes a school likely to help build a mature faith in children, combining the results of many schools in many denominations,[14] gives us nine factors to look for in a good Christian school:

1. a high-quality curriculum that especially includes a quality Bible class and related books;

2. students and teachers who frequently talk with one another about faith;

3. teachers who care about students;

4. teachers, including Bible teachers, competent in their subjects;

13. Hyde, *Religion in Childhood and Adolescence*, 293–94, 334–35.
14. Benson, "Effective Christian Education," 11–22.

5. a sense of school spirit;

6. fair discipline policies;

7. policy that includes student input;

8. student support, encouragement, and rewards from teachers;

9. standards that are consistently enforced.

A second alternative in making a school choice is to homeschool the children. Homeschool associations are quick to proclaim how good these are for children, and plenty of evidence shows that most children do quite well in college after homeschooling.[15] If previously home-schooled students enter public or Christian schools before graduating from high school, they usually do so without a great deal of adjustment. The picture looks quite good, and of course homeschooling provides ample opportunity to influence your children spiritually and to shield them from negative influences that can even exist at Christian schools. Of course some would say that homeschooling gives a sheltered environment that does not equip kids for life in the real world. While such sheltering consequences might possibly occur, our experience with quite a few homeschooling parents suggests that this is rarely the case; home-schooled kids usually are not social misfits when they go to college, and many Christian colleges actively recruit such youngsters because they are often strong leaders with high moral values.

Homeschooling has much to recommend it. One thing to keep in mind about the research on home schools is that people who decide to homeschool their kids are clearly not typical parents. Compared with typical parents, they generally have higher incomes, more college education, and teaching credentials. Further, they are more likely to be two-parent families with only one parent working full time outside the household (and that parent is more likely to have a professional or managerial occupation).[16] Thus a great deal of the positive results of

15. I have seen this personally in my teaching homeschooled children in college, but plenty of research evidence shows this as well. One of the best summaries of the research on home schools is Brian Ray's *Home Schooling on the Threshold*. While this organization is obviously pro-homeschooling, the general research literature tends to confirm the positive results they describe. It is important to note that homeschooling is not just a Christian movement; secular humanists and people of non-Christian faiths also homeschool, although evidence shows that the majority of homeschooling parents today work from Christian assumptions.

16. Ray and Schumm, "Trends in Homeschooling in a Midwestern Community,"

homeschooling may be due to the parents who make this choice, and one might even argue that such kids might do well regardless of where they are educated. But in general, home schools certainly do not hurt kids, and you can customize the education of your children to reflect your values as well as your child's distinctive needs and interests.

We have already made the case for public schools. Our experience with public education was very positive for our daughter in one context and less than ideal in another. Public school for one of our sons was a mixture of good and bad, but probably was better than a Christian school where a bully was allowed to threaten and harm him regularly. We have good friends whose children have had good experiences in public schools, and we know of public schools where most teachers are godly Christians, and the non-Christian teachers are still a generally positive influence on kids. Public school education is, without question, the most popular option among Christians, probably because of less expense and less time required.

We are surprised that more churches do not offer some sort of positive Christian supplement to public-school education. Released-time education can happen when a child is excused during school hours for one or more hours a week for Christian instruction.[17] Legally children must leave the school grounds, but they have lessons that are graded, and the grades may even be recorded by the public school. Released time is a legal option that has consistently been supported by the U.S. Supreme Court of since the 1950s. Yet few parents are aware of this possibility, and fewer churches offer such a program.

In general, released-time programs that are the most successful are those supported by community agencies, we have been told; but several churches might work together to create a strong program. A similar approach that takes less cooperation from schools is an after-school program in a local church. Such programs can provide time for students to do homework while providing some alternative perspectives on faith-related issues.

364–66; Rudner, "Scholastic Achievement and Demographic Characteristics of Home School Students in 1998"; Burns, "A Profile of Selected Characteristics of Arizona's Home Schooling Families."

17. Released-time instruction has a long history in the United States, and was reaffirmed in 1999 by the U.S. secretary of education in a letter to American educators. See Riley, "Guidelines for Religious Education," online: http://www.citizenlink.org/FOSI/education/A000001467.cfm#.

So which do you choose: homeschooling, Christian education, or public education? We used all three options in rearing our children. There are positives and negatives to each. Good Christian schools are often fairly expensive but can be very helpful. But some schools and even some teachers at good schools can be a poor fit for a given student. Homeschooling takes at least one highly motivated and intelligent parent who has the needed time to give to this immense effort. We made use of video-based home-school lessons and felt it was at best a mediocre yet expensive experience. Christian schools and home schools both require considerable financial sacrifice, because of either high tuition or loss of a full-time income. Public schools are often the cheapest and most convenient alternative but can be a positive or negative spiritual influence primarily depending upon the peers your child chooses as friends and on the positive and negative teacher influences.

The answer is . . . Well, it all depends. Your choice depends on the quality of the public schools, Christian schools, and home-school support groups available in your area. The decision you make depends upon your own teaching skills and whether you are emotionally able to spend much of your day with your child (all-day, everyday parenting and teaching certainly is not for everyone). Your decision depends upon the personality and other characteristics of your child, and how well those mesh with the teacher or the school. Of course your decision also depends upon your family resources. We encourage you to make the positive influences on the faith of your child an important consideration in the decision, as you weigh all the factors in this important choice. And don't forget that what works for one child may not work for another, and what works at one age may not work at another. Sometimes it is a matter of trial and error, and sometimes—at the practical level—there is little or no choice. If this is the case, don't feel guilty about it, but monitor the situation closely, get to know your child's teachers personally, get involved in the parent-teacher organization, and be a constructive influence for God's kingdom.

Luminous, Numinous Parenting

G. K. Chesterton is quoted as concluding about schools, "The Christian ideal has not been tried and found wanting. It has been found difficult and left untried."[18] Chesterton's words may indeed summarize much of what this book has been about. Encouraging the spiritual development and experience of the child is far from easy and at times is not very convenient. Most of us prefer the easier alternative when we are given options. But our children's current faith and the preparation for their later faith as well as their eternal destiny should be important considerations—perhaps even the highest priority in our lives and theirs. The Christian parenting ideal is that we surrender most of our concern for self, and that we sacrifice time, money, and energy for the spiritual welfare of our children. But of course to provide them with what they need spiritually, we need to be spiritual healthy as well, and this requires a careful balancing of our emotional and spiritual welfare with that of our children. It is a balance that sounds obviously necessary but can be difficult to achieve in real life.

We should seek to be luminous parents. The dictionary associates *luminous* with a steady light, a light diffused but also bright, enlightening, and inspiring.[19] My study of child development has shown that over and over again researchers speak of the importance of parents' being consistent, dependable, reliable. To be the best possible spiritual influence for our children, we need to seek that ideal of being a steady light. The light need not be dazzling to be effective. Sometimes it is in the background, it is diffused, as we live out life with our child, and then comes to the forefront when needed, at "the teachable moment" when the child asks a question or shares a spiritual experience. It includes the latent influence of regular routines, including faith-related practices in the home and comments during everyday experiences that highlight the work of God in our lives or the beauty of God's creation. But the steady light is bright in the sense that parents do not hedge on the importance of spiritual experiences and of living out the Christian life consistently, regardless of the cost. As parents we should enlighten and inspire our children, both in the special times where the focus in on Christian beliefs and experience, and in mundane life day by day.

Balancing the constant light of being luminous is the need to emphasize and live out the numinous in our lives. The numinous, you will recall, is the sense of the holy, the mysterious, the "otherness" of the

18. Hyde, *Religion in Childhood and Adolescence*, 335, quoting G. K. Chesterton, *What's Wrong with the World?*

19. *New Webster's Dictionary and Thesaurus of the English Language*, 591.

spiritual realm. Even though we may try to package God in convenient ways in our attempts to understand his ways, he is always beyond us. Our understandings are partial, and life gives us experiences in which not understand what God is doing or why he does some things. We need to share with our children this mystery, the sense of the holiness of God, which makes us tremble in awe and wonder at his greatness. Your children have probably experienced that otherness of God already, and they need to know we experience it as well.

To try to be numinous parents, we should walk in the Spirit. The Greek word for "Spirit" in the Bible is *pneuma*, so we might say we shall be "pneumenous" parents. We rely upon the Holy Spirit for direction and redirection. We stay sensitive to his leadings, both when we read Scripture, and when we spend time alone in prayer and meditation before God. The Holy Spirit provides a way for us to share at the deepest levels with our child, because she too can partake of the Source of the numinous, live in the numinous, and thrive in the numinous. Even if our luminous attempts fall short, we can still connect in the numinous of the Spirit.

Of course the terms luminous and numinous do not relate just to spiritual development and experience. Luminous, numinous parenting can infuse other areas of life with our child as well—from gathering around the dinner table to attending a ballgame to approaching discipline. We seek to illumine our child, and we may be illumined in the process. We walk in the numinous of God, whether we sense his mysterious otherness or not, and we affirm God's numinous in our children. Teaching, being taught, and the presence and leading of the Holy Spirit in our lives and those of our children—this should be what parenting is all about.

| TWELVE |

ChildFaith for Parents

Then we will no longer be infants . . . Instead, speaking the truth in love, we will in all things grow up into Him who is the Head, that is, Christ. From him the whole body, joined and held together by every supporting ligament, grows and builds itself up in love, as each part does its work.

(Eph 4:14–16 NIV)

When I was a child, I talked like a child, I thought like a child, I reasoned like a child. When I became a man, I put childish ways behind me.

(I Cor 13:11, NIV)

At that time the disciples came to Jesus and asked, "Who is the greatest in the kingdom of heaven?" He called a little child and had him stand among them. And he said: "I tell you the truth, unless you change and become like little children, you will never enter the kingdom of heaven. Therefore, whoever humbles himself like this little child is the greatest in the kingdom of heaven."

(Matt 18:1–4, NIV)

People were bringing little children to Jesus to have him touch them; but the disciples rebuked them. When Jesus saw this, he was indignant. He said to them, "Let the little children come to me, and do not hinder them; for the kingdom of God belongs to such as these. I tell you the truth, anyone who will not receive the kingdom of God like a little child will never enter it."

(Mark 10:13–15, NIV)

WHEN WE READ THE Scripture passages quoted above, it is easy to conclude merely that we should be humble, trusting God in a childlike manner—but also be mature and not childish. Certainly these ideas are expressed here, but perhaps there is more to these Bible verses. To begin with, what does it mean to "become like little children," and what does "of such is the kingdom" mean to parents? To become humble, for instance, sounds like an active process, not just a personal attribute. Perhaps these first two passages suggest that all God's people—children and adults alike—are on equal ground in some respects. It has been said, "The ground is level at the cross." Have we, as parents, taken this idea seriously in relation to our children? Has the church placed children as high as our other priorities, and does the budget reflect this? Do our family time and family activities reflect that equal ground?

The last two passages call for maturity in the faith; thus being equal to our children before God does not remove our authority and the need to set rules and boundaries. In our being "childlike" we are not given permission to be childish and irresponsible. But the fourth passage also reminds us that we as parents are not alone in the responsibility of spiritual formation.

Most churches practice baptism or child dedication, similar to what Mary and Joseph did when they presented Jesus in the temple when he was nine days old (Luke 2:21–24). A dedication ceremony reflects the belief that children are a gift from God; that while they belong to him, he "loans" children to us for a short while. Our children really aren't ours, even though they came from our union. God has given us the tremendous responsibility to nurture and train them, and to guide them in their relationship with him. As part of a dedication ceremony, churches often pledge their support for parents and affirm their spiritual support for the child. We are intended to have the support of the others in the body of Christ, particularly the fellowship of believers of which we are part. Of course, this presumes the local church reflects the childlike qualities in the first passages above (Matt 18:1–4), by making children equal to other priorities. When the church functions as it should, parents have partners who help in the spiritual nurture of children, and they in turn are also open to learning from children as fellow believers.

The children in the church—the children in our families—will eventually lead the church, or at least we hope so. That leadership is only a few years away, and thus we need to ask, what are we doing to make them strong, kind, capable leaders? and what role do they have today in the church and home that will help prepare them for leadership? My (Don's) own research of preschoolers indicates that even four-year-olds are able to perform church roles such as taking the offering, praying, leading music, and even preaching a short sermon.[1] Such roles can be played out at home, in children's services, and perhaps at least occasionally in congregational worship. Children might give short reports in church of what takes place and what they experience when parents try some of the suggestions in this book. Regular reports by parents and children, espe-

1. Ratcliff, "The Use of Play in Christian Education," 26–33.

cially when they include shortcomings and false starts, may encourage other parents to try similar activities with their children. After several weeks of such reports during the main church service (and other activities that underscore the importance of children's spirituality), it is likely that those attending will realize that children really *are* important to this congregation.[2] But those in the service need to resist the temptation to laugh at cute activities, a response that children often take as laughing at and demeaning the authenticity of spiritual experience itself. How much better for the pastor and others to affirm family-based spiritual formation activities, and reports of spiritual experience by children! Can we really affirm that parents and other adults are equal to children before God if we do not publicly, regularly affirm the value and importance of children's spiritual experiences and activities? Christ himself placed an incredibly high value on children, as seen in his equating children with himself: "Whoever welcomes a little child like this in my name welcomes me" (Matt 18:5; also see Mark 9:37). Can we let children—and their parents—have a few minutes in every church service to talk about spiritual practices and experience in the family, and to encourage other parents to try similar activities? Does the church really love Jesus and thus welcome him in the form of its children? Behind that question, perhaps, is a deeper question: do we really know the love of Jesus?

The Greatest of These

How much do you love your child? Can you recall your feelings when you first saw her or him? What caused you to love your child? When our first child was born, we had eagerly waited for his birth, had agonized over whether we would ever have children after a long bout of infertility, and certainly had loved him throughout the pregnancy. Yet once he was born, we were overwhelmed with the intensity of the love that filled our hearts for this child. We would gladly have given our lives for him. Can anything take this love away? I (Brenda) also recall the extreme vulnerability I felt when our first son, John, was born. I realized instantly that as long as I lived, his little hands would hold my heart; he had the power to crush me when he only weighed eight pounds, four ounces! The love that parents feel for their children is powerful enough to crush the parent. Christians understand God's love for humanity to be even more

2. This process is elaborated on the Web page www.childfaith.net.

intense than the love of parents for their children. Given the extremity of God's love in Christ, many Christians have interpreted Isaiah 53:5 to refer to Jesus's death on the cross, which healed the wound of sin. Isaiah 53:5 states, "He [Jesus] was crushed for our iniquities [sins] . . . and by his wounds we are healed."

Our pastor often asks our small congregation if we really know how much God loves us. With great passion, he exclaims, "God is nuts about you!" The first time we heard him say this we were amused, but it stuck a resonant chord in our hearts. Probably the first childhood song we each learned was the old favorite "Jesus Loves Me, This I Know." But do we really know that he loves us? More important, does that knowledge move from our head to our heart? Do we *feel* his love? Do we walk through the day with joy, resting in the unconditional love of our heavenly Father, or do we continually strive to earn his love?

My (Don's) mother served the Lord all her life. However, she grew up in a very rigid, legalistic religious background, with a father who was too busy in so-called kingdom work to pay attention to his family or even to provide adequately for them. From his perspective, it was relatively easy for an individual to lose salvation, and personal holiness was essential in order to really be in a relationship with a righteous God. My mom apparently thought of God as a stern, judgmental deity, at least at the unconscious level. One could never be certain of his favor and love.

While she was a faithful daughter, loving wife, adoring mother, and committed Christian all her life, she never fully grasped that God *really* loved her, that his love was unconditional and would never be withdrawn. After all, her earthly father had not seemed to love her enough to spend time with her, to provide for her basic needs, or to accept her unconditionally. How could she then expect that God would do more or would love her more than her father had? Two weeks before she died, God completed a work he had begun in her life many years earlier: He somehow—at a deep level surpassing the intellect—convinced her of his abiding and unconditional love. I (Brenda) was privileged to witness this incredible, transformational experience and to hear her, even in a semiconscious state, gasp, "He loves me! Oh, he loves me! I'm so glad, so glad, so glad." Her tears of joy and sense of contentment and peace were precious; her Father, in his mercy and compassion, waited until she grasped a meager understanding of his love before he took her home to be with him.

Sometimes we find it difficult to comprehend the love God has toward us, his children. We cognitively affirm it, and yet in the deepest recesses of our hearts we doubt this love. The overwhelming love we feel toward our children from the moment of their birth is a fuzzy picture of the love that God feels toward us; the fierceness and passion of his love drove him to a cross in the person of Jesus Christ. He chose to lay down his life for us because of the fury of his love. He loves us! He really does; he is indeed nuts about you and me. Ponder this for a moment: the Creator of the universe loves you with utter abandonment. He delights in you and dances over you with joy. His love has no condition attached to it and will never be withdrawn. As the author of *The Shack* could have put it, "God is especially fond of you."[3]

Why is it important to know that you are absolutely loved without reservation? Because it changes everything. We are "no longer a trifling speck in a meaningless cosmos . . . but an eternal creature of infinite worth living in a universe animated by love and care and friendship."[4] Our deep need for love, acceptance, and significance is met in the love of the Father. When we really know that we are loved, we are able to love others as well as ourselves. Our lives take on deeper meaning and God's love flows through us and overflows from us into the lives of those with whom we come in contact. It's not a selfish thing to seek to know the love of God, because it has the power to change lives, both yours and your children's.

What keeps us from truly experiencing this incredible love? For some, believing in God's love is difficult because, like mom, they have had not experienced unconditional love in their families of origin. For others, legalistic teaching and "two thousand years of religious tradition have inculcated in us the mistaken notion that God's love is something we earn."[5] We teach a theology of salvation by grace but live as if salvation depends on our best behavior. Or we believe that God's favor (or lack thereof) is proof of the presence or absence of his love. Remember pulling the petals off a daisy when you were a child while chanting, "He

3. *The Shack*, by William P. Young, has God—as the character called Papa—making a similar statement about many individuals, reflecting the intense, unique affection God has for every person. I sometimes use the phrase "God is especially fond of you" as a personal blessing to my students, because I believe God does have a special affection for each person in their uniqueness as intended from the beginning of time.

4. Smith, *Embracing the Love of God*, xiv.

5. Jacobsen, *He Loves Me!* xiii.

loves me; he loves me not"? The last petal supposedly reveals the truth about whether another returns our love. Unfortunately, many of us play a similar childish game with God, games in which his love is related to our happiness: *I got the raise I needed; he loves me. I lost my job; he loves me not. My children are serving the Lord; he loves me. I have a wayward child; he loves me not.* Since God's favor line always shifts in this scenario, depending on the circumstances of life, we are never quite certain of where we stand with him, or of how he feels about us.[6] God's love seems as arbitrary as the number of petals on a flower.

Fear may also be a hindrance to our really sensing God's love; many of us raised in evangelical Christian homes were literally scared into the kingdom by the fear of hell or of missing the rapture.[7] "Whether we are conscious of it or not, the threat of hell can create an inner dissonance in our perception of the God who seeks our love."[8] Truly knowing the love of God requires that we examine our ideas about who he is and what he wants from us; it requires getting rid of baggage that we may have carried for a very long time, and that is hindering our growth in a love relationship with him.

Some of the fondest memories we have of our children as infants are the experiences of nursing or feeding them. They had no worries about where the milk was coming from, about whether it was warm or cold, or if there was enough to satisfy their hunger. They simply knew that mom or dad was there, and that they would provide what was necessary. Their quiet trust in our ability to provide for them enabled them to relax and be assured of the nourishment their growing bodies needed. Psalm 131 portrays our relationship with God as that of a child at a mother's breast—calm and quieted, resting securely in her love and care. God's invitation to us is to become a child again, to rest in his love and in his ability to care for us and provide for what we need. Amid our worries and concerns over rearing children, God calls us to become childlike once more and to depend upon him.

6. Ibid., 17–18. We highly recommend Wayne Jacobsen's book and are indebted to him for this illustration.

7. We are not dismissing either of these biblical doctrines, although we find it interesting that most often when Jesus spoke of hell, it was in reference to self-righteousness and to highly critical religious leaders of the day.

8. Jacobsen, *He Loves Me!* 19.

Reductionist Parenting

Western society has often bought into a reductionistic model of how the world works. In other words, we tend to see parenting as the input and children's behavior as the resulting output. If the kids make poor choices, there must be something wrong with our parenting. That is the logic, but it is a faulty logic at best. *Reductionism* in this context means reducing the complex influences on children's behavior to parental actions. The truth is that things are always more complex than that. Children are powerfully influenced by the community of which they are a part (including the church community), by their personal choices, and by God. By taking the credit or blame for their behavior, we mistakenly see ourselves as the most important—or sometimes as the only—influence in a child's life. We ought not think more highly of ourselves than we should (Rom 12:3). It is indeed arrogant to think we are the only reason our kids act as they do; this assumption overlooks their free will and disregards a host of other influences.

So don't fall into the trap of believing that if you do everything right in parenting, everything will be fine for your child.[9] If it didn't work for the only perfect parent (God), it won't work for us either! The good news for parents who make mistakes—all of us—is that the general pattern of child rearing has the greatest amount of influence on a child; rarely is a youngster significantly changed by a single negative experience.[10] You will blow it sometimes, but it is comforting to know that it is the day-by-day routines that influence children far more than occasional mistakes.

Yet parenting books don't seem to offer adequate preparation for the times when children disappoint parents or fail to live up to expectations. Have you experienced this? We remember the horror we felt when one of our children, at age two, threw a toy airplane across the room and hit another child in the head. The cries of protest and the pain of the hurt child, as well as the blood running down his tear-stained cheeks, created all sorts of difficult emotions for us. Our reputation as parents was on the line! I (Brenda) used to believe that nurture and

9. Most often cited as a proof-text for this idea is Proverbs 22:6. Yet to take this verse as a promise is to overlook the fact that Proverbs describes tendencies of behavior that may have numerous exceptions. (Ecclesiastes often records those exceptions.) See Osmer's discussion of the diversity of Wisdom in the Bible in *Practical Theology*, 94–96.

10. Kagan, "Family Experiences and the Child's Development," 886–91.

environment were everything, or more simply put, that good parenting always equals good results; bad results must mean that the parents had somehow failed. So if my child behaved poorly or threw an airplane at a friend, then I must have done something wrong. But the Bible paints a very different picture. God, the perfect parent, created a perfect environment for his first children. He loved and nurtured them and yet one hundred percent of the time they have disappointed him and have failed to live up to his expectations. Perfect parenting does not yield perfect children! There are no perfect children, and none of us is capable of perfect parenting!

So what do we do when our children throw airplanes or throw tantrums? What if they become wayward, prodigal from us and from our faith? Does this impact our relationship with God? Do we somehow figure that we have an unspoken bargain with him? *I'll do my best: take them to church, teach them about you; you make sure they turn out all right.* It might sound silly when put that way, and yet many of us live and parent under this unspoken agreement with God. We fear what our children might do; free will is great until it threatens to take our child from the fold of faith into the great unknown. Are you as guilty as we are of looking down on a parent whose child has misbehaved (either in a minor or major way)? We all fear this judgment being visited upon our own household and our own parenting.

I (Don) recall one time (when our two boys were in elementary school) telling them to act better in church, because I had written books on child rearing, and that people might not believe what I said if they acted badly. Almost before the words were out of my mouth, I realized I was asking them to be inauthentic. I was asking them to make me look good. I confess it took me a while to be able to swallow my pride and repent of that statement. A while later I told them that they were much more than the product of my influence. They were unique and valuable, important quite apart from what I may have taught them. I admitted to them that my request was completely self-serving. I did want them to be good, I told them, but not just to make me look good. In fact my reputation should not be the reason why they did or did not do anything. Ultimately my kids and yours will be who they are spiritually. And that's okay. It's okay because before God, we are all wayward sons and daughters.

The Wayward (Prodigal) Son

Jesus told a parable about a man who had two sons; one took his inheritance and left his father's household, the other continued to work for his father in the family business (Luke 15:11–32). We identify the parable as that of the prodigal son, but in reality the parable should be called the parable about the good father. In addition, we often fail to recognize that both sons were prodigals: one became wayward and squandered his father's money; the other refused to enter into a loving relationship with his father but instead worked for him out of a sense of duty and obligation.

So what did the good father do when his younger son left home? First, he allowed his son to make a disastrous choice, even though it cost him dearly. The younger son was saying, "Dad, I'm eager for you to die so I can inherit my portion of your estate." To comply with his son's request required the father to liquidate a significant part of the family farm; consequently "this horrendous family breakdown becomes public knowledge."[11] This was unheard of in the culture of Jesus's time and is not much more acceptable in our culture. The father did not protect his son from the consequences of his chosen lifestyle. We don't read that the father sent a care package to the wayward son in the pigpen! While Dad continued to carry on the affairs of his life, he did so with an eye on the road, with expectancy and hope that his wayward son would return. And there is nothing in the parable that indicates that his faith in God or in his unfailing love was shaken. His reputation in the community might have been shattered, but the portrait Jesus paints is of a man who is steady and unwavering in his faith and in his hope for the future, regardless of what decisions his children make.

Jews during this time had an effective means of punishing any Jewish boy who lost the family inheritance to Gentiles. It was called the *qetsatsah* ceremony and was stricter that the Amish practice of shunning.[12] Whereas shunning disallows eating at the same table as those in the community and restricts the ostracized in other interactions, the *qetsatsah* prohibited any contact whatsoever between the ostracized and any member of the village: separation was total and absolute. When the younger son left his community, he knew that he must not lose the

11. Bailey, "The Pursuing Father."
12. Ibid.

money, but in the parable the son went to a far country and did exactly that (Luke 15:14). According to the *qetsatsah* tradition, if a guilty individual tried to reenter the community, the elders immediately filled an earthen jar with burned nuts and corn. They would carry the jar to the individual, break it in front of him, and the entire community would shout, "This person is cut off from us!"[13] But, the father in the parable formulated a plan for public reconciliation, and so he waited and watched patiently to implement his plan.

Scripture tells us that one day the father saw his son "while he was still a long way off" (Luke 15:20). We can speculate that this father broke the norms for Middle Eastern patriarchy by holding up his long robes as he ran to meet his son. The father prevented public rejection by initiating reconciliation. He cut off his son's attempt at an apology without even mentioning the lost inheritance, and ordered a celebration (Luke 15:20–23).[14] Repentance and reconciliation to his father, his family, his community, and God occurred because of the preemptive actions of the father. Obviously, Jesus's parable was meant to teach his listeners about the love of God. However, it offers much to parents on how to love their children when they go to a "far country." And it is a poignant reminder that we all are prodigals, and all have a Father who is constantly watching for our return to his house—and his heart.

There are no easy answers to the sorrow that the parent of a prodigal experiences. But when we love a prodigal, we become acquainted with God's heart. Isaiah 53 beautifully illustrates the ways that God is acquainted with our sorrows; but by loving (as he loves) children who reject, scorn, and ridicule us, or who blame us for the consequences of their sin, we become acquainted with the sorrow and pain of God's heart.[15] We enter into his suffering. It is important to fully acknowledge and expect that our children will disappoint us in some fashion, such as by childish behavior, by boyhood pranks, by adolescent rebellion, by wayward sexual choices, by unwise selection of partner or career, by drug addiction . . . The list goes on and on. Just as God's own worth

13. Ibid.

14. Ibid.

15. One of the best books we have found on the parable of the prodigal son is Nouwen, *The Return of the Prodigal Son*. We were tempted to try to include some of his rich insights here, but it is much better to get them firsthand by reading that book. What is included here, some of which overlaps with Nouwen's ideas, is the product of Brenda's independent study on this topic.

and value as a parent cannot be judged by the actions of his children, so neither should ours. Our worth and value is affirmed by our Father's love for us, not by how our children act. Our task is to love as we have been loved: unconditionally. If our children engage in actions contrary to what we have taught them, we must continue to love them. If they are still under our roof, we must discipline appropriately—but must always love lavishly, furiously and unconditionally.

The danger in any how-to book on parenting is that the reader will go away with a supposed formula for success. In actuality, there are no guarantees in parenting; we do the very best we can, but the results are not under our control. Our children have the power to choose their course in life, just as we do. We hope and pray that they make right choices as they enter adulthood. When they do, we will rejoice. When they don't, we will affirm their freedom to choose but expectantly hope and wait for their return. Sometimes the hardest thing we are called to do is to watch someone struggle, yet not interfere. This is particularly difficult when that someone is our child. But struggles can produce good fruit in time, so we wait and pray expectantly.

You are indeed very fortunate if your children never do anything more foolish than throw an airplane across the room. We are not suggesting that you expect the worst to happen, but rather that you pray daily for your kids, faithfully teach and train them, and affirm them as persons. If they make choices that break your heart, do not lose faith or allow their behavior to impact your love for them or your relationship with your Father. He grieves with you, loving them even more than you do.

Conclusion

We hope you have discovered some ideas in this book that resonate with you and your child, and have begun to try out some of them. We are certain you will come up with additional ideas that will uniquely help your child in the journey towards the Father's heart and ultimately to heaven. Just as important, we hope you have adjusted the ideas you use so they fit you and your children.

Our goal has been to help you nurture your child's loving relationship with God. But it is also important for you to consider your own relationship with the Father. After all, the quality of that relationship with God will influence your child's. To a great extent, faith transmission occurs by example, which may be one of the reasons the Ten Command-ments speak of the "sins of the fathers" being evident in the children for three or four generations (Exod 20:5). What is often overlooked is that the same passage—the very next verse—affirms that we can turn from our hostility to God, that we can pass on the love that God freely offers, and that the effects will last for a *thousand* generations! We will fall short, but when we admit this fact about our own lives, our children can see our own child faith in action. When we ask God's forgiveness—and ask forgiveness from our children when we wrong them—they see authentic, personally owned faith in action. Children are more likely to believe and claim as their own an authentic faith that they can see. But, again, there is no guarantee. And, regardless of your parenting, they too will come up short of perfection. Our prayer is that together you and your children will continue on this amazing spiritual journey, and that together you will continually discover the riches of fully knowing God and his love for you.

| Bibliography |

Aldridge, Jerry, and Jean Box. "Moral and Affective Dimensions of Childhod." In *Handbook of Children's Religious Education*, edited by Donald E. Ratcliff, 82–101. 1992. Reprint, Eugene, OR: Wipf & Stock, 2008.

Augustine, *Confessions*. Translated with an introduction by Henry Chadwick. Oxford: Oxford University Press, 1991.

Arrington, French L., and Roger Stronstad, editors. *Life in the Spirit New Testament Commentary*. Grand Rapids: Zondervan, 1999.

Bailey, Kenneth E. "The Pursuing Father." *Christianity Today*, January 26, 1998. Online: http://www.christianitytoday.com/ct/1998/october26/8tc034.html/.

Balmer, Randall. *Mine Eyes Have Seen the Glory: A Journey into the Evangelical Subculture in America*. 4th ed. Oxford: Oxford University Press, 2006.

———, producer. *Mine Eyes Have Seen the Glory: A Journey into the Evangelical Subculture in America*. Public Broadcasting Service. 1989. DVD. Worcester, PA: Vision Video, 1992.

Benson, Peter L. "Effective Christian Education: A Synthesis of Recent Denominational Studies." *Journal of Research on Christian Education* 1 (1992) 11–22.

Berryman, Jerome W. "The Chaplain's Strange Language: A Unique Contribution to the Health Care Team." In *The Chaplaincy in a Children's Cancer Center*, edited by Jan Van Eyes, 15–40. Austin: University of Texas Press, 1985.

———. *The Complete Guide to Godly Play*. 7 vols. Harrisburg, PA: Morehouse Education Resources, 2002–2008.

———. *Godly Play: A Way of Religious Education*. San Francisco: HarperSanFrancisco, 1991.

———. *Teaching Godly Play: The Sunday Morning Handbook*. Nashville: Abingdon, 1995.

———. "Religious Images, Sick Children and Health Care." In *Children in Health Care: Ethical Perspectives*, edited by Sally A. Francis and the Association for the Care of Children's Health, 19–31. Washington, DC: Association for the Care of Children's Health, 1981.

———. "The Rite of Anointing and Pastoral Care of Sick Children." In *The Sacred Play of Children*, edited by Diane Apostolos-Cappadona, 63–77. New York: Seabury, 1983.

Boyatzis, Chris J. "The Co-construction of Spiritual Meaning in Parent-Child Communication." In *Children's Spirituality: Christian Perspective, Research, and Applications*, edited by Donald Ratcliff et al., 182–200. Eugene, OR: Cascade Books, 2004.

Bunge, Marcia, Terrence Fretheim, and Beverly Robets Gaventa, editors. *The Child in the Bible*. Grand Rapids: Eerdmans, 2008.

Burns, Patrick Curtis. "A Profile of Selected Characteristics of Arizona's Home Schooling Families." EdD diss., Northern Arizona University, 1993.

Bushnell, Horace. *Christian Nurture.* 1847. Reprint, New York: Scribner, 1912.

Buzzelli, Cary A., and Kevin Walsh. "Discipline, Development, and Spiritual Growth." In *Handbook of Children's Religious Education,* edited by Donald E. Ratcliff, 143–63. Birmingham, AL: Religious Education, 1992.

Campolo, Anthony, and Donald E. Ratcliff. "Activist Youth Ministry." In *Handbook of Youth Ministry,* edited by Donald E. Ratcliff and James A. Davies, 257–74. Birmingham, AL: Religious Education, 1991.

Cavalletti, Sofia. *The Religious Potential of the Child.* Translated by Patricia M. Coulter and Julie M. Coulter; preface by Jerome W. Berryman. New York: Paulist, 1983.

Coles, Robert. *The Moral Life of Children.* Boston: Houghton Mifflin, 1986.

———. *The Spiritual Life of Children.* Boston: Houghton Mifflin, 1990

Coles, Robert, et al. *Listening to Children: A Moral Journey with Robert Coles.* DVD. 2007. Originally recorded in 1995. Durham, NC: Duke University Center for Documentary Studies. Social Media Productions. Alexandria, VA: PBS Home Video, distributor.

Cram, Ronald Hecker. *Bullying: A Spiritual Crisis.* St. Louis: Chalice, 2003.

Csikszentmihalyi, Mihaly. *Flow: The Psychology of Optimal Experience.* New York: Harper & Row, 1990

Curran, Dolores. *Traits of a Healthy Family: Fifteen Traits Commonly Found in Healty Families by Those Who Work with Them.* San Francisco, Harper & Row, 1984.

Dobbins, Richard. "Too Much Too Soon." *Christianity Today,* October 24, 1975, 99–100.

Dobson, James C. *Dare to Discipline.* Wheaton, IL: Tyndale House, 1980.

Edersheim, Alfred. *Sketches of Jewish Social Life.* Originally published 1876. Updated ed. Peabody, MA: Hendrickson, 1994.

Engel, James F., and H. Wilbert Norton. *What's Gone Wrong with the Harvest? A Communication Strategy for the Church and World Evangelization.* Grand Rapids: Zondervan, 1975.

Erikson, Erik H. *Childhood and Society.* New York: Norton, 1950.

Feinberg, Jeffrey Enoch. "Foundation for Leadership and Messianic Education (FLAME)." Web site. Online: http://www.flamefoundation.org/.

Foster, Richard J. *Celebration of Discipline: The Path to Spiritual Growth.* Rev. ed. San Francisco: Harper & Row, 1988.

Fowler, James W. *Stages of Faith: The Psychology of Human Development and the Quest for Meaning.* San Francisco: Harper & Row, 1981.

Fuller, Cheri. *Opening Your Child's Spiritual Windows: Ideas to Nurture Your Child's Relationship with God.* Grand Rapids: Zondervan, 2001.

Gaede, S. D. *Belonging: Our Need for Community in Church and Family,* Grand Rapids: Zondervan, 1985.

Hay, David, with Rebecca Nye. *The Spirit of the Child.* Rev. ed. London: Kingsley, 2006.

Hayes, Edward L. "Evangelism of Children." In *Childhood Education in the Church,* edited by Robert Clark, et al., 399–415. Rev. and exp. ed. Chicago: Moody, 1986.

Hayford, Jack W. *Blessing Your Children.* Ventura, CA: Regal, 2002.

Hess, Valerie E., and Marti Watson Garlett. *Habits of a Child's Heart: Raising Your Kids with the Spiritual Disciplines.* Colorado Springs: NavPress, 2004.

Hopkins, Mary Rice, "How to Lead Music with Kids." In *Children's Ministry that Works! The Basics and Beyond,* edited by Craig Jutila, et al,. 114–20. Rev. and updated ed. Loveland, CO: Group, 2002.

Howe, Neil, and William Strauss. *Generations: The History of America's Future, 1584–2069.* New York: HarperPerennial, 1992.

———. *Millennials Rising: The Next Great Generation.* New York: Vintage, 2000.

Hyde, Brendan. *Children and Spirituality: Searching for Meaning and Connectedness.* London: Kingsley, 2008.

Hyde, Kenneth E. *Religion in Childhood and Adolescence: A Comprehensive Review of the Research.* Birmingham, AL: Religious Education, 1990.

Imber-Black, Evan, and Janine Roberts. *Rituals for Our Times: Celebrating, Healing, and Changing Our Lives and Our Relationships.* New York: HarperPerennial, 1992.

Ingle, Clifford, editor. *Children and Conversation.* Nashville: Broadman, 1970.

Issler, Klaus. "Biblical Perspectives on Developmental Grace for Nurturing Children's Spirituality." In *Children's Spirituality: Christian Perspectives, Research, and Applications,* edited by Donald E. Ratcliff et al., 54–71. Eugene, OR: Cascade Books, 2004.

———. *Wasting Time with God: A Christian Spirituality of Friendship with God.* Downers Grove, IL: InterVarsity, 2001.

Jacobsen, Wayne. *He Loves Me! Learning to Live in the Father's Affection.* Newbury Park, CA: Windblown Media, 2007.

Kagan, Jerome. "Family Experiences and the Child's Development," *American Psychologist* 34 (1979) 886–91.

Kasdan, Barney. *God's Appointed Customs: A Messianic Jewish Guide to the Biblical Lifecycle and Lifestyle.* Baltimore: Lederer, 1996.

———. *God's Appointed Times: A Practical Guide for Understanding and Celebrating the Biblical Holy Days.* Rev. ed. Baltimore: Lederer, 2007.

Lawson, Kevin. "In Right Relationship with God: Childhood Conversion in Evangelical Christian Tradition." In *Nurturing Child and Adolescent Spirituality: Perspectives from the World's Religious Traditions,* edited by Karen-Marie Yust, et al., 108–21. Lanham, MD: Rowman and Littlefield, 2006.

LeFever, Marlene. *Creative Teaching Methods: Be An Effective Christian Teacher.* Rev. ed. Colorado Springs: Cook Ministry Resources, 1996.

Lightfoot, Cynthia. *The Culture of Adolescent Risk-Taking.* Culture and Human Development. New York: Guilford, 1997

Lingo, Susan. *Written on Our Hearts: Helping Children Understand, Memorize, and Retain God's Word.* Grand Rapids: Zondervan, 1995.

Lozoff, Bo. *It's a Meaningful Life: It Just Takes Practice.* New York: Penguin Compass, 2001.

Madsen, Erik C. *Youth Ministry and Wilderness Camping.* Valley Forge, PA: Judson, 1982.

Mains, Karen. *The God Hunt: The Delightful Chase and the Wonder of Being Found.* Downers Grove, IL: InterVarsity, 2003.

———. *Making Sunday Special.* Nashville: Star Song, 1994.

Marty, Martin E. *The Mystery of the Child.* Religion, Marriage, and Family. Grand Rapids: Eerdmans, 2007.

Massey, Claity P. "Preschooler Moral Development." In *Handbook of Preschool Religious Education,* edited by Donald E. Ratcliff, 82–100. Eugene, OR: Wipf & Stock, 2008.

May, Scottie, et al. *Children Matter: Celebrating Their Place in the Church, Family, and Community.* Grand Rapids: Eerdmans, 2005.

McDannell, Colleen. "Creating the Christian Home: Home Schooling in Contemporary America." In *American Sacred Space,* edited by David Chidester and Edward Linenethal, 187–219. Religion in North America. Bloomington: Indiana University Press, 1995.

McLaren, Peter. *Schooling as a Ritual Performance: Towards a Political Economy of Educational Symbols and Gestures.* 2nd ed. London: Routledge & Kegan Paul, 1993.

Mecum, Shelly, et al. *God's Photo Album: How We Looked for God and Saved Our School.* San Francisco: HarperSanFrancisco, 2001.

Meier, Paul D., and Donald E. Ratcliff. *Raising Your Child: From Birth to Twelve.* Grand Rapids: Spire, 1999. Online: http://www.don.ratcliffs.net/raisingchild/part1.pdf/ and http:www.don.ratcliffs.net/raisingchild/part2.pdf/.

Montagu, Ashley. *Touching: The Human Significance of the Skin.* 3rd ed. New York: Perennial Library, 1986.

Montessori, Maria. *The Child in the Church.* St. Paul, MN: Catechetical Guild, 1965.

New Webster's Dictionary and Thesaurus of the English Language. Danbury, CT: Lexicon, 1992.

Nordeman, Nichole, with accompanying musicians. "Who You Are." In *Recollection: The Best of Nichole Nordeman.* Audio compact disc. SPD 78635. Brentwood, TN: Sparrow Records, 2007.

Nouwen, Henri J. M. *The Return of the Prodigal Son: A Story of Homecoming.* 1st Image Books ed. New York: Doubleday, 1994.

Okagaki, Lynn, et al. "Socialization of Religious Beliefs." *Journal of Applied Developmental Psychology* 20 (1999) 273–94.

Osmer, Richard R. *Practical Theology: An Introduction.* Grand Rapids: Eerdmans, 2008.

Otto, Rudolf. *The Idea of the Holy: An Inquiry into the Non-Rational Factor in the Idea of the Divine and its Relation to the Rational.* 2nd ed. New York: Oxford University Press, 1950.

Pascal, Blaise. *"Pensées" and Other Writings.* Translated by Honor Levi; with an introduction and notes by Anthony Levi. The World's Classics. Oxford: Oxford University Press, 1995.

Piaget, Jean. *Six Psychological Studies.* Translated by Anita Tenzer and David Elkind. Edited with an introduction and notes by David Elkind. New York: Random House, 1967.

Potok, Chaim. *The Chosen: A Novel.* New York: Simon & Schuster, 1967.

Pottebaum, Gerard A. *The Rites of People: Exploring the Ritual Character of Human Experience.* Rev. ed. Washington, DC: Pastoral, 1992.

Ratcliff, Brenda. "Water, Stones, and Bones: Thoughts on My Pilgrimage to Israel." Online: http://www.brenda.ratcliffs.net/stonesbones.pdf

Ratcliff, Donald E. "Baby Faith: Infants, Toddlers, and Religion." *Religious Education* 87 (1992) 117–26.

———. "Children's Spirituality: Christian Perspectives." Online: http://www.childspirituality.org/

———, editor. *Handbook of Children's Religious Education.* Eugene, OR: Wipf & Stock, 2008.

———, editor. *Handbook of Preschool Religious Education.* Eugene, OR: Wipf & Stock, 2008.

———. "Parenting and Religious Education." In *Handbook of Family Religious Education,* edited by Blake J. Neff and Donald Ratcliff, 61–86. Birmingham, AL: Religious Education, 1995.

———. "Peer Culture and School Culture Theory: Implications for Educational Ministry with Children." *Christian Education Journal* 4 n.s. 1 (2000) 57–76.

———. "Rituals in a School Hallway: Evidence of a Latent Spirituality of Children." In *Christian Education Journal* 5 n.s. 2 (2001) 9–26.

————. "Rituals in a School Hallway: Evidence of Latent Spirituality in Children." Online: http://eric.ed.gov/ERICWebPortal/contentdelivery/servlet/ERICServlet? accno=ED457460/; and http://www.childfaith.net/resources/.

————. "Stages of Spiritual Development: Crisis Experiences in the Christian Life." *Christian Education Journal* 14 (1993) 73–86. Online: http://www.don.ratcliffs.net/ books/stages.pdf

————. "Stories, Enactment, and Play." In *Handbook of Preschool Religious Education*, edited by Donald E. Ratcliff, 247–69. Eugene, OR: Wipf & Stock, 2008.

————. "Temperament in Childhood: Three Key Dimensions: Activity, Emotionality, and Sociability." Online: http://www.don.ratcliffs.net/conferences/temper.pdf/.

————. "The Use of Play in Christian Education." *Christian Education Journal* 6 (1985) 26–33.

Ratcliff, Donald E., et al., editors. *Children's Spirituality: Christian Perspectives, Research, and Applications.* Eugene, OR: Cascade Books, 2004.

Ray, Brian. *Home Schooling on the Threshold: A Survey of Research at the Dawn of the New Millennium.* Salem, OR: National Home Education Research Institute, 1999.

Ray, Brian, and Walter Schumm. "Trends in Homeschooling in a Midwestern Community." *Psychological Reports* 82 (1998) 364–66.

Riley, Richard A. "Guidelines for Religious Expression in Public Schools." Republished by Mark A. Fey. Online: http://www.citizenlink.org/FOSI/education/A000001467 .cfm#/.

Religion News Service. "Clergy Ratings at Lowest Point Ever." *Christianity Today*, January 22, 2003. Online: http://www.christianitytoday.com/ct/2003/002/12.21.html/.

Rizzuto, Ana-Maria. *The Birth of the Living God: A Psychoanalytic Study.* Chicago: University of Chicago Press, 1979.

Roehlkepartain, Eugene C. *The Teaching Church: Moving Christian Education to Center Stage.* Nashville: Abingdon, 1993.

Rudner, Lawrence M. "Scholastic Achievement and Demographic Characteristics of Home School Students in 1998." *Education Policy Analysis Archives* 7 (March 23, 1999). Online: http://epaa.asu.edu/epaa/v7n8/.

Schwartz, Kelly Dean, et al. "Mentors, Friends, and Gurus: Peer and Nonparent Influences on Spiritual Development." In *The Handbook of Spiritual Development in Childhood and Adolescence*, edited by Eugene Roeklkepartain, et al., 310–23. The Sage Program on Applied Developmental Science. Thousand Oaks, CA: Sage, 2006.

Smalley, Gary, and John Trent, *The Gift of the Blessing.* Updated and expanded ed. Nashville: Nelson, 1993.

Smith, James Bryan. *Embracing the Love of God: The Path and Promise of Christian Life.* San Francisco: HarperSanFrancisco, 1995.

Solary, Scott, and Luci Westphal, directors. *All God's Children.* DVD. New York: Good Hard Working People, 2008.

Spiceland, J. D. "The Numinous." In *Evangelical Dictionary of Theology*, edited by Walter A. Elwell, 783. Baker Reference Library 1. Grand Rapids: Baker, 1984.

Stafford, Wess, with Dean Merrill. *Too Small to Ignore: Why Children Are the Next Big Thing.* Colorado Springs: Waterbrook, 2005.

Stonehouse, Catherine. *Children's Worship.* VHS videotape. Wilmore, KY: Asbury Theological Seminary Information Technology Department, 2000 (author's copy). Segment Online: http://childfaith.net/stonehouse.html/.

————. *Joining Children on the Spiritual Journey: Nurturing a Life of Faith.* Grand Rapids: Baker, 1998.

Berryman. *Young Children and Worship*. Louisville: Westminster John Knox, 1989.

Stewart, Sonja M., and Jerome W. Berryman. *Young Children and Worship*. Louisville: Westminster John Knox, 1989.

Tamminen, Kalevi, et al. "The Religious Concepts of Preschoolers." In *Handbook of Preschool Religious Education*, edited by Donald E. Ratcliff, 59–81. Eugene, OR: Wipf & Stock, 2008.

Thomas, William I., and Dorothy S. Thomas. *The Child in America: Behavior Problems and Programs*. New York: Knopf, 1928.

Thompson, Marjorie J. *Family: The Forming Center; A Vision of the Family in Spiritual Formation*. Nashville: Upper Room Books, 1989.

Troup, Richard, and J. Omar Brubaker, "Recreation and Camping for Children." In *Childhood Education in the Church*, edited by Robert Clark, et al., 307–30. Rev. and exp. ed, Chicago: Moody, 1986.

VonSeggen, Dale, and Liz VonSeggen. "Puppets and Presentations that Connect with Kids." In *Children's Ministry that Works!: The Basics and Beyond*, edited by Craig Jutila, et al, 121–35. Rev. and updated ed. Loveland, CO: Group, 2002.

Wallinga, Charlotte, and Patsy Skeen. "Physical, Language, and Social-Emotional Development." In *Handbook of Preschool Religious Education*, edited by Donald Ratcliff, 30–57. Eugene, OR: Wipf & Stock, 2008.

White, W. "Family." In *The Zondervan Pictorial Dictionary of the Bible*, 2:496–501. Grand Rapids: Zondervan, 1975.

Wilkinson, Bruce H. *Experiencing Spiritual Breakthroughs*. Sisters, OR: Multnomah, 1999.

———. "Leaving a Legacy." In *A Life of Integrity: 13 Outstanding Leaders Raise the Standard for Today's Christian Men*, edited by Howard G. Hendricks, 131–46. Sisters, OR: Multnomah, 1997.

Winnicott, D. W. *Playing and Reality*. London: Routledge, 2005.

Young, William P. *The Shack: A Novel*. Newbury Park, CA: Windblown Media, 2007.

Yount, Christine. *With All Their Heart: Teaching Your Kids to Love God*. Chicago: Moody, 2002

Zimmerman, Martha. *Celebrating Biblical Feasts in Your Home or Church*. Minneapolis: Bethany House, 2004.

Zuck, Roy B. *Precious in His Sight: Childhood and Children in the Bible*. Grand Rapids: Baker, 1996.